An Invi

Lunch

by Joy David

**PUBS
HOTELS
WINE BARS
RESTAURANTS
INNS**

♦ **Sights to see**
♦ **Places to visit**
♦ **Things to do**

In Somerset, Avon and Gloucestershire

including chapters on:
Exmoor National Park, Bristol,
The Cotswolds

Edited by Emma Macleod-Johnstone
The Author and the Editor wish to thank the team
for their enthusiasm, humour and hard work in
helping to compile this book: Sheila Burns, Adrian
Carey, Hilary Kent and Mervyn Wilcox.

Thanks are also given to
Emma Macleod-Johnstone and Louise Robson
for all the drawings.

The Hanging Chapel, Langport, Somerset

ISBN 1-873491-10-7
First published 1991
© Joy David
All rights reserved

Typeset by Exe Valley Dataset Limited, Exeter, Devon
Printed and bound in Great Britain by
R. Booth Bookbinders

CONTENTS

INCLUDES:

*"When you have lost your inns, drown your empty selves,
for you will have lost the last of England."*
Hillaire Belloc

Somerset, Avon and Gloucestershire

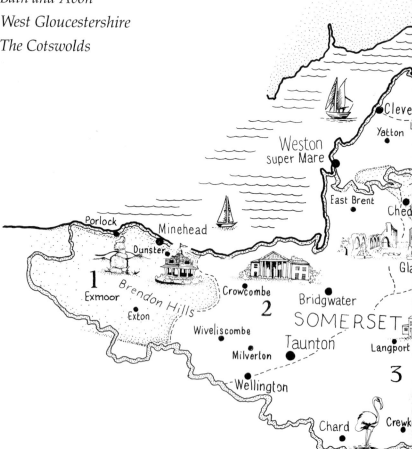

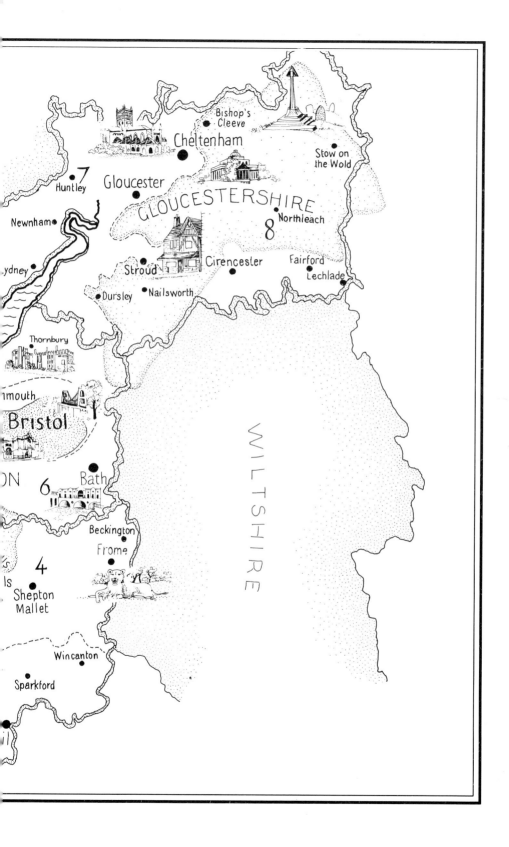

AN INVITATION TO LUNCH, DINE, STAY & VISIT
IN SOMERSET, AVON AND GLOUCESTERSHIRE

INTRODUCTION

It was a family discussion about where we should go for lunch on the Sunday before Christmas that prompted the writing of this series of books. I though we knew the local area well enough to make it a fairly simple choice but when it came down to brass tacks this was definitely not the case.

We did not mind whether it was a hotel, a restaurant or a good pub but with the gathering of the clan for the festive season, the group's demands were somewhat exacting. It had to be somewhere that children were welcome and grannies would not be out of place; the men wanted a decent pint of Real Ale and to be well fed. Log fires, old beams, and a good malt Scotch were added to the list with the request for provision of some kind of activity after lunch, to help one's system limber up for the annual Christmas gorge. Either a scenic walk near the venue if the weather was kind or an indoor entertainment if it were not, and to add to this ever growing list of requirements, one of our number was a vegetarian.

Having got together all the ingredients that were required to make a successful outing the question still remained unanswered. Where?

We dug out old newspapers, looked through Yellow Pages but not once did we discover, listed, the information that we sought. Finally we did find a super pub, had an excellent lunch and walked for awhile on the moors; but what an effort!

This book has been designed to help you find easily a suitable establishment to answer your needs, whether it be for lunch, dinner, stay or visit. Some are simple down to earth pubs, others are more sophisticated but every venue has its own dedicated page which tells you exactly what you can expect in the way of food, the sort of establishment it is, the opening hours, if they take credit cards, have access for the disabled, if children are welcome and if there is a garden.

The beginning of every chapter is devoted to what there is to see and do around the pubs, restaurants and hotels. Some places you will know, others may be new.

This is an all the year round book, as pertinent in summer as in winter. Useful to couples looking for somewhere different, families, and perhaps a secretary wanting to find somewhere for her boss to take a visiting client.

I have tried to make sure there is something for everyone which is almost an impossibility but I hope that readers will be kind enough to write to me and tell me about their favourite spots so that they can be included in the next edition.

The timeless Packhorse Bridge, Allerford, Minehead

INCLUDES:

*"Tis not the eating,
Nor 'tis not the drinking that is to be blamed,
but the excess."*
John Seldon

Exmoor straddles the borders of Devon and Somerset with a determination to be recognised for its own worth and not solely as a part of either county; a place of magical beauty, enchanting vistas, and not a little sinister in parts. Its villages are timeless and, once visited, it will always beckon you back to discover more. The word moor suggests it is inland but this is not so of Exmoor; part of its grand beauty is its coastline, where every twist of the road will give you a sometimes tantalising glimpse through the leaf laden branches of trees to the sparkling sea, and at other turns of your path you will be left gasping at the sheer clarity of the ocean splendour. The coastline takes the full force of the winter's gales which are ferocious and menacing but to the well wrapped onlooker, the frightening majesty sends the adrenalin coursing through the body.

In 1954 Exmoor became a National Park, somewhere to be protected for future generations. Its wild magnificence has been recognised and the ever increasing number of people who fall under its spell each year, seem to have harmonised with those lucky enough to live here, establishing a code which simply underlines the need, for everyone who loves Exmoor, to be responsible for its future.

For many of us, our first introduction to Exmoor was the story 'Lorna Doone', written by R.D. Blackmore in the late 19th century. So powerful is his description of Exmoor that I have always found it hard

Lorna Doone Cottage

*to believe that it is fiction. Visit the tiny church of St Mary, at **Oare**, where Lorna was shot on her wedding day; feel the wonderful atmosphere envelop you; take note of the plaques on the wall and you, like me, will want to believe the Doones and the Ridds did exist. The church with its medieval wagon roofs is open daily during daylight hours. It is odd to think that this beloved book almost faded into insignificance when it was published. It was not until Queen Victoria's daughter, Princess Louise, became engaged to the Marquis of Lorne that it became a best seller. Why? Because an over zealous and misinformed critic wrote in his column that the book was about the ancestors of the Marquis. From that moment it became the fashionable thing to read 'Lorna Doone'.*

*   **Combe Martin**, boasting the longest village street in England, is the stepping stone into Exmoor from the west. Apart from the wonderful views, it has one of the strangest pubs in the area, THE PACK OF CARDS so called because of a 17th-century gambler, George Ley who won a vast sum of money at cards and decided to use his ill-gotten gains to build the house. It was built with four floors, each representing one suit. Each floor has 13 doors for the 13 cards in each suit and the whole building has 52 windows.*

*   Dominating the parish and rising over a thousand feet from the sea are the Hangman Hills, which mark the western boundary of the National Park leading you to the superb scenery, the exotic red deer and the sturdy Exmoor ponies. The village is famous for its Hobby Horse ceremony, the Hunting of the Earl of 'Rone at the Spring Bank Holiday, and the Carnival in the first week of August. There is the excellent COMBE MARTIN WILDLIFE PARK here, farm parks, a motor cycle museum and wonderful walks.*

*   **Lynton** and **Lynmouth** are linked together by a remarkable CLIFF RAILWAY which opened in 1890. It climbs 500ft above sea level along a 900ft track. Worked by water and gravity it must have seemed terrifying to the intrepid users when it first started, they never having seen anything like it before. Sir George Newnes was the driving force behind its construction because he saw the need for easier access between the two villages which had grown in popularity during the Napoleonic wars when the English were unable to travel abroad. Lynmouth is a gem; the River Lyn runs through Lynton and tumbles over moss strewn rocks and boulders, through thickly wooded hills as it falls to the sea at Lynmouth. The village has a picture postcard quality and where better to enjoy it than a stay at THE RIVER LYN VIEW or THE RISING SUN where Blackmore is said to have written most of Lorna Doone, Shelley spent his honeymoon with his child bride, and Robert Southey dreamed. Lynmouth would inspire anyone who is not without soul. Its*

quieter neighbour, Lynton, has its own charm and within the comfortable doors of THE ROYAL CASTLE HOTEL *you will find a warm and cheerful welcome.*

I look forward to trips on the last sea-going paddle steamer in the world, the famous WAVERLEY, *and the traditional cruise ship* BALMORAL *which sail on day trips, afternoon and evening cruises from* **Minehead, Lynmouth** *and* **Ilfracombe.** *As you sail into Ilfracombe remember this nice story. In 1797 four French ships were sighted off the port. Most of the towns 200 full time-sailors were away serving with the Royal Navy. The women folk recognised that they were in imminent danger of being invaded. With ingenuity and courage they removed their traditional red petticoats and draped them round their shoulders like scarlet cloaks, then took up prominent positions on high ground around the town. The French spotted them through their telescopes and believing the red cloaks meant the town was garrisoned with a large number of military, set sail with alacrity. The cruises provide a unique way to view the whole of the magnificent Exmoor coast: sail away to Wales or see* **Lundy Island** *and the Devon coast. For more information ask at the Tourist information Centres or ring (0446) 720656.*

There are some wonderful walks between Lynmouth and Combe Martin. Some are for experienced walkers only but no one should miss the sheer splendour of the Valley of the Rocks. Leave Lynmouth from Riverside Road with the RHENISH TOWER *on the right, cross the road to turn left by the pavilion where there is a signpost 'To the VALLEY OF THE ROCKS'. It winds uphill to join the path to the north of Hollerday Hill called* NORTH WALK, *a path cut to the Valley of Rocks by a Mr Sanford in 1817. It is a brilliant feat of engineering. The first time I walked it, I spent much of the time bewitched by the scenic beauty and the sight of the Welsh coast. At times the path drops sheer away to the pounding sea below. The colouring is fantastic; rocks and boulders are covered with lichen, the mixture of colours heightened where the dark patches of ground ivy curl around tree stumps. Eventually the eye reaches the rock masses of Ragged Jack and Castle Rock guarding the entrance to the Valley of the Rocks. The Valley was created during the Ice Age some 10,000 years ago - awe inspiring.*

Do you like Brass Rubbing? If you do, the EXMOOR BRASS RUBBING AND HOBBYCRAFT CENTRE *in Watersmeet Road, Lynmouth, will give you hours of pleasure. There is no entry charge, you merely pay for your rubbing. The prices start from £1.35 with over 100 brasses and children's rubbing plates of Kings, Queens, Knights, Clergy, Skeletons, Exmoor scenes, Children's stories, Animals, Oriental*

Dancers and a 'No-Smoking sign! Open normally from Monday to Friday, but 7 days a week from Easter during school holidays and half terms until the end of September plus the Autumn half-term, from 10.30am-5.pm.

The National Trust owns WATERSMEET now but once it belonged to the Hallidays. He was the heir to a merchant's fortune who fell in love with the wild beauty of this north-western corner of Exmoor and began buying land in the early part of the 19th century. He and his wife were philanthropists who planned to set up a patriarchal estate, peopled with tenants for whom they laid out farms and provided employment. This romantic couple built a dream mansion beside the sea at Glenthorne, two miles east of Countisbury, with a drive plunging ever more steeply from County Gate, 1,000 feet above, at the border of Devon and Somerset. In 1832 they constructed WATERSMEET HOUSE, in an equally romantic setting. It now accommodates the Trust's restaurant, shop and information point. Watersmeet is glorious, one of two places in Britain where the Irish spurge is found. Revelling in the damp, clean air so close to the sea, lichens, mosses and ferns abound, creating a site of national importance for ancient woodland flora.

*Strictly speaking, **South Molton** is not in Exmoor but we may be forgiven for mentioning it because it makes a wonderful springboard for exploring all that Exmoor has to offer. It is an ancient sheep and cattle market town dating back to the 12th century. Until the 19th century it thrived as a centre of the wool trade. Today it is quietly charming with its fine Georgian houses and a nice early 15th-century parish church, St Mary Magdalen which you approach along an avenue of limes. For 300 years THE POLTIMORE ARMS, situated between South Molton and Simonsbath, has been caring for travellers. A hospitable, friendly inn which serves food 7 days a week until 9.30pm. An ideal place for refreshment perhaps after visiting the SOUTH MOLTON MUSEUM which is housed in a 17th-century building. A fascinating place with a wealth of interesting displays including 18th-century wig making tools, cider presses and a wooden fire engine.*

*HANCOCK'S DEVON CIDER at **Clapworthy Mill**, in the beautiful Bray Valley, is also well worth a visit. Apart from being able to buy scrumpy, cider, honey and cream from the shop there is also a Craft shop. You will be invited too to see their video film and colour photo exhibition on cider making. It is open Monday to Saturday 9-1pm, 2-5.30pm (closed on Sundays).*

Many people have found great pleasure in visiting QUINCE HONEY FARM in North Road, South Molton: acknowledged by experts to be the World's best Honeybee exhibition. It is an all weather attraction and is open daily from 9am-6pm October-Easter.

A visit to ARLINGTON COURT should always be on your agenda when you are in this part of the country. Just 7 miles north east of Barnstaple, it will always give the visitor intense pleasure. It is by no means the most prepossessing of houses, quite severe in fact, and its exterior will certainly not prepare you for the amazing Victorian clutter inside: collections of all manner of articles, gathered together by the last occupant, Miss Rosalie Chichester who lived here for eighty four years before her death in 1949. Miss Chichester was an extraordinary woman who travelled the world. She struggled to keep Arlington going – her father had been a spendthrift and left her with debts which would have terrified most people and sent them scurrying to the Bankruptcy Courts.

Tarr Steps, Exmoor's famous Clapper Bridge

Not this courageous lady however. Her determination to hold on to Arlington never wavered; it meant that the estate was neglected however, and when the National Trust took it over major restoration was needed and fortunately has been carried out splendidly. The grounds are a joy; there is an excellent exhibition of carriages. The house has been sorted out but not denuded of Miss Rosalie's treasures. I love the rather angry looking red amber elephant from China which stands in pride of place in the White Drawing room. Her passionate devotion to all things living, whether plants or creatures, led her to allow her parrots to fly free in the house, causing irreparable damage to the curtains! On the first floor landing you can see a watercolour of her favourite parrot, Polly. The Jacob Sheep and Shetland ponies in the park are descendants of those she established as part of a wildlife refuge.

THE EXMOOR FOREST HOTEL in **Simonsbath** *is an ideal stepping stone on your way to discover the wild, stark beauty of Exmoor. I cannot say that the village excites me for it does not but it is a wonderful foil to the exquisite scenery which surrounds it on every side. However, within the welcoming walls of the Exmoor Forest Hotel you can plan expeditions to the many wonderful places nearby, like TARR STEPS perhaps. This is one of the finest examples of a clapper bridge: large flat stones placed across the tops of upright stones, that you will see anywhere. These clapper bridges date from medieval times and are still withstanding the test of time. A very popular spot and although there is plenty of parking the approach road tends to get a bit congested. TARR STEPS FARM will provide you with excellent morning coffee, lunch and cream teas.*

The villages of Exmoor hide in the valleys and combes and **Withypool** *is no exception. It has a church with a round Norman font; the ROYAL OAK INN which has been renowned for its food and hospitality for three hundred years, and now THE WESTERCLOSE COUNTRY HOUSE HOTEL AND RESTAURANT which offers just about anything one could want for either a meal or a visit. To stay there would be to give you chance to absorb some of the history of this ancient village. For example there is a STONE CIRCLE on the westward slope of Withypool hill which dates from the early Bronze Age and still has 30 or 40 of the upright stones standing. The fine old bridge is one of four crossing the River Barle, the other three are at Simonsbath, Landacre and Dulverton. Landacre bridge is in a moorland setting. There are car parking spaces and some wonderful riverside walks. The name Withypool derives from the sound of the willows rustling along the waters of the Barle. It is a wonderful place to stay, you can fish for salmon or trout, ride or enjoy the spectacular walks all around.*

The woods and hills of Exmoor close round **Dulverton** *on three sides, the Barle flows past its front doorstep. It is a place steeped in history and one of tranquillity. In the church are two memorials to the Sydenhams who lived from 1540 to 1874 at Combe, a beautiful Tudor House. Here Drake married Elizabeth Sydenham and it could well be that the two Armada medals found under the porch of the church were left there by the great man. A visit to THE ANCHOR INN afterwards will not only refresh you but you will find the staff willing to answer as many questions about the area as you care to ask. If you are in Dulverton* *in the spring take a walk in Burridge Woods which becomes totally carpeted with bluebells.*

*The A398 from Dulverton will take you through superb country-side to **Dunster**, at the west gate of Exmoor. It seems to belong to centuries past. It is unforgettable; a place to savour and about which to dream. DUNSTER CASTLE rises dramatically above the village and the sea. It dates from the 13th century and for over 600 years it has been the home of the Luttrell family. Colonel Luttrell gave it to the National Trust in 1975 and we are privileged in being able to visit it. The gardens and grounds are wonderful especially the terraces where rare shrubs grow. The church is unique. It is two-in-one, the Monks' Church and the Peoples' Church dating back 500 years. In the High Street is the YARN MARKET, a quaint octagonal building erected in 1609 when wool was made into cloth in this area and kerseymere, a fine twill cloth of local wool, was marketed here. I can sincerely recommend two excellent places to stay, OSBORNE HOUSE HOTEL and DUNSTER CASTLE HOTEL. For good food at anytime of the day you will find THE CASTLE COFFEE HOUSE just down from the Castle has something for every-one. Dunster has a quiet unspoilt beach which is totally safe for children and has the great advantage of being the only beach you can drive onto in West Somerset. It also has one of the most valuable places for tourists. THE EXMOOR NATIONAL PARK'S NEW VISITOR CENTRE.*

All visitors to Exmoor have a basic need for information about the area, but the role of effective information and interpretation goes beyond this. Encouraging visitors to take an interest in their surroundings may help them enjoy their stay more, to develop a greater awareness of conservation and management issues, and to respect the interest of those who live and work within the Park. This is done mainly through information centres and publications but also, and effectively, through direct contact between visitors and the National Park Authority Ranger Service and others, informally and on organised events.

In the mid 1960's the Authority operated only two information centres and provided a limited range of literature concentrating upon waymarked walks. By the late 1970's, four manned information centres, at Dulverton, County Gate, Lynmouth and Combe Martin attracted a total of 40,000 visitors per annum. By relocating the Lynmouth centre and opening a fifth permanent centre at Dunster, the throughput has risen to almost 500,000. In addition, visitor contacts have been maintained 'out of hours' through computerised information systems, and a mobile information unit has toured local shows which take place throughout the summer months. The free information newspaper, the 'Exmoor Visitor' introduced in 1985, has proved a popular medium both for the visitor and the local tourist providers who advertise in it. It has brought together a range of information about the Park which is seen by two thirds of all visitors to Exmoor.

It is really the Visitor's Centre in Dunster that I wanted to tell you about, before I got sidetracked. Dunster thrived in medieval times on the woollen industry. An eye-catching feature here draws attention to it. There are 30 metres of wool woven, exactly to the style of the medieval cloth, from almost 30 miles of yarn, supplied by Craftsman's Mark of Wellington, the proprietor of which, Morfudd (pronounced Morveth) Roberts, also supervised the production of the cloth. The Yarn was woven at COLDHARBOUR MILL at **Uffculme***, itself a museum of wool production and well worth visiting. Setting up the loom took several days and involved tying many hundreds of knots by hand before weaving could start.*

One length of the cloth has been left in its natural, slightly grubby looking, state. This would be virtually identical to the woollen cloth worn by the monks of nearby CLEEVE ABBEY in the 13th century. Further lengths of the unique reproduction medieval materials have been dyed by Gill Dalby, a local specialist in the use of vegetable dyes. Indigo was used to create the blue; madder, the red; and weld, the yellow.

The invitation to the visitor very definitely is 'please touch'.

In 1500, many of the homes in Dunster would have had a spinning wheel where the housewife and the unmarried daughters would have toiled ceaselessly for all the daylight hours. Their efforts would have earned them little more than a penny a day. An independent weaver would have kept a team of about five or six women fully employed spinning yarn to meet his needs. This woven cloth was washed and taken out to the Castle Tor to be dried in the open air at the Tenteryarde. It was stretched tight on Tenterframes by means of Tenterhooks. Now you know where the expression 'to be on Tenterhooks' comes from. I certainly did not know this before. Another term came into being as well. When using a spinning wheel, women (never men) drew the fibres from the distaff. This women's work has resulted in the 'distaff side' to indicate the female side of a family.

In the Visitor's Centre, a mounted Exmoor Horn ram – representing the source of wool – presides over the imaginative interpretation of the processes involved in producing woollen cloth in Dunster in 1500.

On quiet days, if there are any in this fascinating place, Dunster born Beryl Priddle, who is in charge of the National Park's Visitor's

Centre, may find time to demonstrate to visitors the spinning of wool on a traditional spinning wheel.

Without question the Exmoor Visitor's Centre is a great boon to visitors and it could not be better situated than in Dunster. The story the Centre tells will give visitors an insight into so many things and into the history of Dunster which will heighten their enjoyment of this lovely place.

*There is one corner of **Minehead** where a steep flight of steps takes you up to the church of St Michael. It is quite charming and reminds me so much of scenic Clovelly. Until you have been to Minehead you cannot appreciate what a delightful place it is. Protected by the hills which rise behind it, the houses have flowers climbing up over their doors and walls, it is still a little old-fashioned which is part of its charm. The people are courteous as you will find out when you visit THE OWLS RESTAURANT or THE HOBBY HORSE INN. THE WEST SOMERSET RAILWAY gives you a touch of nostalgia as you ride along the scenic way to **Bishops Lydeard**.*

Cottage with bread oven in Stony Street, Luccombe

Porlock Vale stretches from Porlock Weir, the tiny harbour nestling beneath the wooded cliffs of Porlock Hill and Bossington, near Hurlestone Point, to the hills of Tivington and Selworthy. Within the Vale lie the villages of **Porlock, Bossington, Lynch, Allerford, Horner, Selworthy** and **Luccombe**. You can walk, ride, sail, fish or just relax. Marshlands in the sweeping bay offers rewarding walks. It is an *area rich in nice old pubs, quaint shops and the romance of the moorland history. Nowhere better can be found to round off this tour of Exmoor than THE LORNA DOONE HOTEL which is actually in Porlock. It epitomises the hospitality of this unsurpassed territory.*

THE CASTLE COFFEE HOUSE

Restaurant and Coffee House

4, High Street,
Dunster, Somerset
Tel: (0643) 821 219

The Castle Coffee House nestles in the shadow of Dunster Castle, an excellent destination after the steep descent from its turrets. Carol and Brian Hedger for the past three years have been the owners of this delightful Elizabethan building, instigating many changes, none in anyway detrimental its age or olde world decor.

The Hedgers, realising that the traveller or the holidaymaker frequently loses track of time, serve a full menu all day. Delicious cream teas, or a full meal, or just beverages can be enjoyed at any time. They serve specialist coffees, fresh ground and beans, and with the increasing popularity of specialist and herbal teas many will be delighted to know that these are also served. Both the latter and ground coffee are sold to take away.

In the summer the tea garden is open for soft ice cream, drinks and snacks. The whole of the first floor is a roomy salad bar seating 40 people in a pleasant Regency setting providing cold meats, salads, gateaux, sweets and drinks; good, plain home-made cooking at reasonable prices. During the season a traditional roast is served on Sundays and everyday there are dishes for vegetarians. Victorian dress is worn by the staff on the May Bank Holiday and also on the first Friday and Saturday evenings in December for the Dunster Candlelight Festival: a collaborative effort by all the villagers with candles placed in every window, period costumes, and folk dancing in the streets. The atmosphere has to be experienced first hand, a warning though: it is addictive.

USEFUL INFORMATION

OPEN: Sum:9.30am-10pm
   Win:10am-5.30pm
CHILDREN: High chairs, baby
   changing facilities
CREDIT CARDS: Access/Visa/
   Master/Euro
LICENSED: Full Restaurant Licence
GARDEN: Tea Garden in summer.
   Dogs welcome
**Customer Pay Phone

RESTAURANT: Good, plain English
   Fare
BAR FOOD: Not applicable
VEGETARIAN: Always available
ACCESS FOR THE DISABLED:
   Ramp. Toilet.

High Street
Dunster, Somerset

Tel/Fax No: (0643) 821445/812558

DUNSTER CASTLE HOTEL
Hotel

This wonderful 8 bed-roomed hotel takes its name from the Norman Castle which overlooks the Medieval village of Dunster. The picturesque village has a 12th-century Priory Church, a 16th-century Yarn Market, which was built for the sale of cloth when Dunster was a small port, and a 17th-century working Water Mill. It is located in the beautiful countryside of the Exmoor National Park, close to the west Somerset coast and 25 miles from the M5.

Dunster Castle Hotel is a listed building thought to be 400 years old, tastefully restored, and the car park was once the walled kitchen garden of the Castle. Adjoining the hotel is a Victorian Ice Cream Parlour, where period dress is worn, and a traditional Candy Store. There is a garden bar, serving fruit wines, and a cold buffet of local meats and pies, as well as traditional cream teas; a cellar bar serving Somerset Cider and a selection of real ales and bar snacks. This bar and the hotel were recently featured in an episode of the Agatha Christie series, Poirot. The food is imaginative and delicious with specialities such as Rabbit Casserole, Chicken and Pork Cobbler, fresh locally caught plaice and trout, and a particularly good home made lasagne. The A La Carte menu includes beef in red wine, Entrecote Bordelaise, Pasta Margarita and Sirloin Steak Garni amongst its many dishes. Bar Food is equally as good, if simpler. You can choose from Steak Baps, Steak and Kidney Pie or perhaps Peggies, a local vegetable pastie. The Childrens Menu delights the young. At the Weekend there is a traditional Carvery Sunday lunch.

USEFUL INFORMATION

OPEN: 8am -11pm
CHILDREN: Welcome in Res't, Garden & Hotel
CREDIT CARDS: Access/Visa/ Amex/Diners
LICENSED: Free House. Full licence
GARDEN: Scenic garden – evening 'Bar-B-Ques' & Jazz nights are held

RESTAURANT: A la Carte menu
BAR FOOD: Traditonal country fare
VEGETARIAN: Several dishes
ACCESS FOR THE DISABLED: Yes

OSBORNE HOUSE
Hotel and Restaurant

31 High Street,
Dunster, Somerset.
Tel: (0643) 821475

This is a fitting hotel and restaurant for this lovely medieval village. Osborne House is at the top of the High Street, in sight of the castle, facing the 16th century Yarn Market with a backcloth of superb countryside. Full of character, this charming house dates back in part to the 17th century. There is nothing nicer than sitting at a table in the bay window of the restaurant eating delicious food, a glass of wine in your hand and a wonderful view as the finishing touch.

Ann Cook is the owner of Osborne House and this dedicated lady has a team of friendly efficient people working with her both in the hotel and the restaurant. In the twelve months that Ann has been here she has made many changes in all areas. Bedrooms have been redecorated and are looking very pretty. The restaurant has had a new carpet and a subtle facelift and much energy and imagination has been put into the menus and the range of fare produced in the Osborne House kitchen.

From the Coffee Shop lunch menu you can have anything from filled Jacket Potatoes, Omelettes and Grills, to Pasta and Rice Dishes. Snacks are available all day and the cakes and gateaux will tempt anyone with a sweet tooth. The evening menus in the restaurant are slightly more sophisticated with super choices from the a la carte including the house specialities, Duck Osborne, individual Beef Wellingtons and a good selection of vegetarian dishes, whilst the 4-course Table d'Hote offers excellent value at a set price. On Sundays a traditional lunch is available for which booking is advisable.

USEFUL INFORMATION

OPEN: 10.30-5.30pm 6.45-9pm last orders
CHILDREN: Welcome
CREDIT CARDS: Visa/Access/ Eurocard/Mastercard
LICENSED: Wines, Spirits & some beers
GARDEN: No

RESTAURANT: Excellent range & quality
BAR FOOD: Not applicable
VEGETARIAN: Dishes every day
ACCESS FOR THE DISABLED: No

Exebridge,
Dulverton, Somerset.
Tel: (0398) 23433

THE ANCHOR INN
Inn, Hotel & Restaurant

No one could possibly be made more welcome than at The Anchor Inn, Exebridge. It lies close to Oakford, just south of where the rivers Barle and Exe join up on the edge of Exmoor. The inn is around 300 years old and it was here that the famous highwayman of Exmoor, Tom Faggus, was seized and later hanged at Taunton. His mount, Winnie, was shot in the stable which is now the resident's lounge.

The River Exe renowned for its trout and salmon flows past the Anchor's garden and makes it the ideal place for fishermen to stay. Talk in the bar is almost always of fishing, hunting, walking or shooting, although visitors also want to know about the 'Lorna Doone' countryside. Look for the 'Lorna Doone' trail signposts.

Mr and Mrs Phripp, the owners and their staff could not be more friendly people, whose attitude is 'nothing is too much trouble', and who are always willing to tell you about local history. You can dine in style every day, or lunch on Sundays, in the renowned Stableblock Restaurant from an a la carte menu which is the epitome of all that is best in home cooking and hard to beat for standards and value for many a mile. The Bar menu is equally enticing and the wine list superb. The Anchor Inn is full of old-world charm and a delight to visit.

USEFUL INFORMATION

OPEN: Hotel: all year Rest: 7-9.30pm, Bar: 12-2.00, 6.30-10pm
CHILDREN: Yes, in Riverside Lounge
CREDIT CARDS: Visa/Mastercard/ Eurocard/Access
LICENSED: Full licence. Ushers beers, Doone ales, Good wines
GARDEN: Grounds overlooking river. Marquee tables outside, childrens play area.

RESTAURANT: Full a la carte. The very best of home cooking
BAR FOOD: Extensive menu daily
VEGETARIAN: 2 dishes on each menu
ACCESS FOR DISABLED: No, but easy access

RIVER LYN VIEW
Hotel

26 Watersmeet Road,
Lynmouth, Devon
Tel: (0598) 53347

One can almost envy anyone who sees Lynmouth for the first time. Not for nothing is it known as the 'Little Switzerland' of England because of the steep hills which lead down to this riverside harbour village. In the 1960s this pretty place suffered a devastating flood which took a toll of life and the scars still remain, but life goes on and the resilience of the people have made sure that visitors are welcome in this lovely area. It is a paradise for naturalists and walkers, fishermen drool over their catches, poets and artists never lose an chance to visit. The River Lyn Hotel offers you the opportunity to stay or just to eat and drink in delightful surroundings.

The hotel is approximately 200 years old and was built as watchmen's cottages. It was converted in the 1950s and still retains many original features including unexpected doorways and winding staircases. It is a small establishment which means that you can expect excellent personal service ensuring that all visitors leave with satisfied appetites and pleasant memories of the food and the small team who comprise the staff.

At lunch time there is a wide selection of home-cooked bar snacks, in the afternoon cream teas are available and at night you can dine from the table d'hote menu or settle for an excellent bar snack. Sandwiches and Gateaux are available all day and on Sundays there is an excellent three course traditional lunch.

USEFUL INFORMATION

OPEN: Lunch: 11.30-2pm Teas: 3-5pm
  Eve. Meals: 6.30-9.30pm
CHILDREN: Families welcome
CREDIT CARDS: Streamline
LICENSED: Restaurant & Residential
GARDEN: None

RESTAURANT: Table d'hote incl.
  venison, local salmon/trout
  specialities in season
BAR FOOD: From prime steaks –
  home-made quiches
VEGETARIAN: One or two dishes
ACCESS FOR THE DISABLED:
  Level entrance

Castle Hill,
Lynton, North Devon.
Tel: (0598) 52348

THE ROYAL CASTLE HOTEL
Hotel/Inn

This delightful hotel enjoys what must be one of the finest locations in North Devon, bordering on Somerset. It is 500ft above sea level and has wooded slopes which lead down to the old village of Lynmouth. The spectacular views are magnificent looking out over the Bristol Channel, South Wales coast, the Lyn Valley and many other beauty spots from the Bar, Restaurant, Terraces and most of the main bedrooms. It is small wonder that in the past the Hotel was patronised by King Edward VII, when he was Prince of Wales, and other members of the Royal Family and nobility.

Retaining the atmosphere of an Edwardian country house, with many interesting local and historical pictures of the period, the Royal Castle Hotel provides all modern facilities and is just the place for anyone seeking peace and tranquillity in comfortable and elegant surroundings, whether it is to come here for some excellent food or just to stay. Special Autumn/ Winter mini breaks are available including bed, breakfast and dinner, they are marvellous value and worth enquiring about.

There is a wide range of Bar Meals and snacks available at lunchtimes and an A la Carte menu in the evenings, seven days a week all the year round. The menu changes daily and in the Bar you can sample the Chef's specials which are displayed on the blackboard behind the bar. There are all the usual things including a variety of first class Ploughmans with crispy bread. The restaurant offers a more formal atmosphere and choice with something to suit everyone, with a complementary and very fine wine list; vegetarian meals will be prepared upon request. Traditional lunches are served on Sundays during the winter months.

USEFUL INFORMATION

OPEN: All the year, last orders 9.00pm
CHILDREN: Welcome
CREDIT CARDS: None
LICENSED: Full Licence
GARDEN: Terraces. Sea views

RESTAURANT: Excellent menu
BAR FOOD: Wide choice. Daily specials
VEGETARIAN: On request
ACCESS FOR THE DISABLED: Yes.

THE HOBBY HORSE INN

Public House

The Esplanade,
Minehead, Somerset.
Tel: (0643) 702274

Tony and Barbara Saunders are the proprietors of this interesting inn, which is an end wing of a marvellous Victorian building that was once the Grand Metropole Hotel. The name, Hobby Horse, comes from the Sailors Hobby Horse, which parades the streets of Minehead from sun rise on May day preceded by a lively accordion band. It is a sight well worth seeing. The pub could not be more conveniently situated, right on the sea front with views across the Channel to Wales, it is within sight of the Golf course and Somerwest World Holiday camp, and 150 yards away is the privately owned West Somerset Steam Railway. If its shops which you seek, then they are virtually round the corner.

Before they came to the Hobby Horse six years ago, the Saunders were at the Golf Club and so they know the area well, as do their staff, all willing to advise on what to see and where to go. Ballroom dancing takes place every Tuesday evening and visitors are welcome.

Although there is a small dining room available, most people prefer to eat either in the bar or in the large garden on a summer's day. There is a daily Table d'hote menu with fresh vegetables and poultry. The home made sweets tempt everyone who sees them. The A la Carte menu offers a selection of succulent steaks, mixed grills, fish, salads and vegetarian dishes. Children's meals are available and so are a wide selection of freshly cut sandwiches and rolls. Sunday lunch is very popular throughout the year and you need to arrive early to be sure of a seat. It is a nice, wholesome, friendly establishment which is a pleasure to visit.

USEFUL INFORMATION

OPEN: Coffee: 10.30-12noon Lunch: 12-2pm
CHILDREN: Back room & garden not bar
CREDIT CARDS: None taken
LICENSED: Full Licence
GARDEN: Large garden

RESTAURANT: Wide choice, good food
BAR FOOD: Daily specials home cooked
VEGETARIAN: 4 dishes
ACCESS FOR THE DISABLED: Yes

THE OWLS RESTAURANT

Restaurant

1c The Avenue
Minehead, Somerset.

Tel: (0643) 707131

Anne and Geoff Clayton own and run The Owls Restaurant above the shops in the main street leading up from the sea front. This nice, spacious restaurant is a popular venue for locally held functions. Food is served all day starting at 8am, Sundays 10.30am. Normally they close at 5pm but from Easter to autumn they are open 6.30 – 9.00pm with a superb evening menu.

There is a six page daytime menu, so it would be difficult not to find something you enjoy. The prices are sensible and this is very true. A traditional English breakfast which is served all day and includes tea or coffee costs just £3.35. There are Jacket Potatoes with all kinds of fillings, 4-Egg Gourmet Omelettes, and that is without starting on the main meals of the day. Fish, of course, is included and so are home-made Steak & Kidney Pies, Lasagne, Quiche, Chicken Curry and other dishes. Pizzas are freshly baked and made to order, and there are super sandwiches.

Lunch always includes a roast and, quite frequently, turkey as well. Anne claims that traditional crispy Yorkshire pudding can be guaranteed. All the roasts are served with roast or new potatoes, and vegetables. You are equally welcome to just drop in for coffee or afternoon tea. To book ring 707131 or Just 'Pop-In

USEFUL INFORMATION

OPEN: 8am-5pm. Sunday: 10.30am.
Easter-Autumn: 8am-9.30pm
CHILDREN: Welcome
CREDIT CARDS: Access/Visa
LICENSED: Yes
GARDEN: Not applicable.

RESTAURANT: Traditional, home-cooked food at sensible prices
BAR FOOD: Not applicable
VEGETARIAN: Always available
ACCESS FOR THE DISABLED: One flight of stairs

THE LORNA DOONE HOTEL

Hotel

High Street, Porlock,
Somerset TA24 8PS
Tel: (0643) 862404

This fine, ten bedroomed hotel is one of the most comfortable and best managed in North Devon. Situated right in the centre of Porlock it makes an ideal base from which to enjoy the plethora of delights in the surrounding area: the many beautiful walks on Exmoor; the coastal path and the sea are less than a mile away. The fascinating twin villages of Lynton and Lynmouth with their Victorian Cliff Railway are just ten miles distant, and Minehead six miles.

It is an interesting hotel with quite a history. The Earl of Lovelace, nephew of the poet Lord Byron, had it built in 1886 on the site of the old Three Horseshoes Inn; the original stables and coachman's house still surround the cobbled court-yard at the rear of the building.

One of the attractions of the Lorna Doone for both non-residents and residents is the availability of food all day, every day in the Coffee Shop or Restaurant. Toni and Dick Thornton, the proprietors, have given much care and thought to the compilation of their quite original menus even to producing one specially for Vegetarians. The extensive range of fare offered includes some standard favourites but it is the unusual, beautifully presented recipes that guarentee the hotel's increasing popularity. On Sundays a 3 course lunch is available for £5.95 with a choice of 3 starters, 3 main courses (including one roast and one vegetarian), plus sweets. The emphasis is always on home prepared food using fresh produce. It is a delightful venue and once having experienced its warmth and hospitality, you will want to return as so many people have before you.

USEFUL INFORMATION

OPEN: Coffee Shop 10.30am-5pm
Restaurant: 7.00pm-9.15pm
CHILDREN: Welcome
CREDIT CARDS: Visa/Mastercard
LICENSED: Restaurant/Residential
GARDEN: Patio area
**Bed & Breakfast from £16.50pppn

RESTAURANT: Fresh/original home prepared dishes
BAR FOOD: Not applicable
VEGETARIAN: 5 main courses
ACCESS FOR THE DISABLED: Level access

Simonsbath
Nr. Exford. Somerset.
Tel: (064) 383 341

EXMOOR FOREST HOTEL
Hotel, Restaurant & Free House

Set in a superb area of natural beauty the Exmoor Forest Hotel offers just about everything one could wish for. There are rolling hills and long valleys with rivers and streams in abundance. The hotel owns seven miles of fishing rights to delight any fisherman and for those who want to walk the choice is endless. The people of Exmoor will tell you that there is no better way of seeing the countryside than horse riding and this too is available.

Exmoor Forest Hotel was once two cottage some 400 years ago and then the front section was joined on in the early 19th century. It has a wonderful atmosphere and its years of hospitality are being carried on now by the owner, aided by his staff and 'Aunt Mary', a charming ghost, who owned the hotel in the early 1900s and has stayed ever since making sure that everything is up to scratch! Neither she or the visitors are ever disappointed.

The choice of food is excellent with seasonal venison, pheasant, rabbit, prawns and local trout much in evidence. If you like sauces you will be in your element. Of course not everything is served with a sauce but every dish is cooked to perfection. On Sundays there are always two different roasts and everyday the Bar has a wide selection of home-cooked food plus super sandwiches and a choice of Ploughmans. Exmoor Forest Hotel also has its own tearooms in which you can indulge in a wonderful cream tea after taking a brisk walk to make room having eaten such a healthy lunch.

USEFUL INFORMATION

OPEN: Win: 11-2.30pm, 6.30-11.00pm
    Sum: 11-11.00pm
CHILDREN: Welcome
CREDIT CARDS: Access/Visa
LICENSED: Full on License + Supper
GARDEN: Front Lawn & Patio

RESTAURANT: Top Class A La Carte
BAR FOOD: Wide Choice,Home
    made dishes etc
VEGETARIAN: 3 or 4 dishes daily
ACCESS FOR THE DISABLED:
    Level entrance

THE POLTIMORE ARMS
Inn

Yarde Down,
South Molton, Devon
Tel: (0598) 710381

In a wonderful situation, 1000 ft up on Exmoor, way off the beaten track yet only 7 miles north of South Molton and 12 miles from Barnstaple, The Poltimore Arms is a delightful inn. On a clear day the views are stunning, you can see Hartland Point and Lundy beyond it. On a summer Sunday the village cricket pitch resounds to the sounds of bowlers and batsmen. It is the ideal venue for anyone wanting to get away from the stress of everyday living.

For over 300 years the Poltimore was a packhorse staging post, and served both Royalist and Parliamentary forces in the Civil War of 1642-6. It has a ghost named Charlie who may well have been in occupation since then. He is mischievous fellow who has been known to boil a kettle and regularly moves artefacts. Ten years ago a pixie was caught in the bar in the Exmoor Pixie Hunt! Apart from the fun and the welcoming hospitality, Mike and Mella Wright are ideal innkeepers. The well being of their customers comes first.

Mella is the chef and produces delicious meals. Her home-made turkey pie is very popular and so are the various daily specials available. The bar and the restaurant menu are quite extensive and it would be very difficult not to find something to tempt the taste buds. There is a menu for children, one for vegetarians and even Vegans are specially catered for. In summer there are Barbeques in the garden under cover. If there are more than 8 of you pre-bookings are preferred.

USEFUL INFORMATION

OPEN: 11.30-2.30pm. 6-11.00pm Sun:12-2pm, 7-10.30pm Food to 9.30pm all week
CHILDREN: Garden & Games room
CREDIT CARDS: None taken
LICENSED: Cotleigh Tawny Bitter. Full Wine list
GARDEN: Yes. Barbeques in summer

RESTAURANT: Home made country fare. A La Carte evenings
BAR FOOD: Wide range. Home made & take away
VEGETARIAN: 3 dishes + Vegan
ACCESS FOR THE DISABLED: Yes

WESTERCLOSE COUNTRY HOUSE
Hotel and Restaurant

Withypool,
Somerset.
Tel: (064383) 302

Five minutes walk from the village, set in its own fields, Westerclose Country House has stunning views over the surrounding countryside. It was built in 1928 as a hunting lodge for the Nicholson family, producers of the well known gin.
It is a wonderful place to stay either to enjoy a break or join in one of the organised Walking or Birdwatching weekends in the Spring and Autumn.

Withypool nestles in a hollow in the heart of the Exmoor National Park. Food is one of the pleasures of the walking week-ends. The group has a splendid picnic lunch, returns to the hotel for tea and scones with clotted cream. Afterwards a bath, a change of clothes and perhaps a drink before a candle lit dinner. Riding is one of the principal pastimes on Exmoor and guests are able to use the facilities of the hotel's stables on request. The hotel is open to non residents and what better place to lunch or dine. There is a choice of table d'hote or a la carte menus.

The traditional English, West Country and Vegetarian dishes are prepared with skill and imagination using locally produced fresh fish, meat and cream. Most vegetables are grown in the hotel's kitchen garden. There is a comprehensive wine list and catering for those on special diets is no problem. Packed lunches and light snacks are available on request. The conservatory bar is a delight; beautiful views across the fields to Withypool Hill, and doors leading to a flagstone patio and garden.

USEFUL INFORMATION

OPEN: All year. Res't: Mon. residents only. Lunch 12.30-2.30pm Tea: 3.30-5pm. Dinner: 7.30-9.30pm
CHILDREN: Welcome. Chairs, cots etc Childrens meals from 6pm onwards
CREDIT CARDS: Access/Visa/ Amex
LICENSED: Full restaurant licence
GARDEN: Patio with tables & chairs.Lawns

RESTAURANT: English & West Country recipes
BAR FOOD: Upon request
VEGETARIAN: Always available
ACCESS FOR THE DISABLED: Yes.

The Church of St. Mary Magdelene, Taunton

INCLUDES:

". . . When Love is dead
Ambition fled
And Pleasure, lad, and Pash,
You'll still enjoy
A sausage, boy,
A sausage, boy, and mash."
A.P. Herbert

NORTH WEST SOMERSET

*The North West of Somerset is a wonderful area of exploration. The coast line encompasses the whole of Bridgwater Bay: with the little, romantic port of **Watchet** on its western flank, and the quietly beautiful **Brean Down** on the other side. Inland, there is everything from the market town of **Wellington** to the county town of **Taunton**. The M5 moves through the centre and rather than detracting from the scenery it has enhanced it besides making a lot of small places easily accessible.*

*At Watchet the harbour is so small that you wonder how any craft can safely manoeuvre in and out. This was the port where Coleridge first conceived the 'Ancient Mariner'. I love coming here having first had a good lunch at THE GEORGE in **Nether Stowey**. For a small place Nether Stowey has a lot going on, not least the QUANTOCK SHEEP MILKING CENTRE where you can see sheep being milked, and even milk one yourself if you wish. There are young lambs to touch and hold, a variety of other small animals and a delightful walk along what is described as The Stowey Woods Woodland Experience. It is open Sundays and Wednesdays from March – mid July and then daily until mid September.*

Then there is COLERIDGE COTTAGE across the road from the appropriately named 'Ancient Mariner' pub. Coleridge lived here for three years with his wife and infant son. He loved the cottage and wrote some of his best poems here. You can see his massive inkstand, locks of his hair and some of his letters. There are pictures of the village in Devon where he was born, the church where he was married, and the room in Highgate where he died.

The Quantocks are an unspoilt area of peace and quiet for anyone who loves the countryside. They are best explored on foot and always it is gentle hill walking with quiet combes reaching from Taunton to the coast near Watchet.

*From Watchet take the B3188 road towards **Wiveliscombe** and you will come to COMBE SYDENHAM COUNTRY PARK at **Monksilver**. This historic country estate which was rescued from total disrepair in 1964 by the Theed family, is a very special place. Throughout the park you have the unique opportunity to see the Theed's 40 year restoration plan in action; from 400 year old trout ponds, recently re-dredged and stocked, to the West wing of the Hall where the Courtroom has recently been completed. This room has to be seen for you to understand the owners' passion for preserving the past for the future. All the family will enjoy the 'Alice' and 'Tree' story trails which take you* on a celebration of nature through the Country Park. These trails are not just walks but an awareness of the countryside. Combe Sydenham opens from the end of March until the 1st November, Sunday to Friday 10am-5pm.

Lunch, after a visit to nearby GAULDEN MANOR which is lovely, could well be taken at the THE BARON OF BEEF, **Hillcommon** which is almost equi-distant between Wellington and Taunton.

Gaulden Manor

You may look up to Wellington's monument standing high on a spur of the Blackdown Hills, and wonder what it is doing there. It all comes down to the hero of Waterloo. He seems to have decided on Wellington as his title, when he was made a duke, without any personal connection with the town. Wellington honoured by his choice which brought them instant fame repaid the compliment by building the duke a column, 175ft high. It was meant to be crowned with a figure of the great man, and to be the centre of a group of cottages for Waterloo pensioners. Sadly, it was too expensive a scheme for the town which for years found the upkeep of the column with its hundreds of steps a big drain on its budget. There was great relief when it was taken over by the National Trust. Recently it has had a face lift and is beautifully illuminated at night. I must warn you though that the climb up to it is daunting and not for the feeble.

The beautiful and timeless parish church in Wellington is descended mostly from the 13th and 14th century, and the east window is about 700 years old. Sir John Popham lies here surrounded by his family. He was the man who sentenced Sir Walter Raleigh to death. I am amazed that he had the temerity when his own character is not without stain. He was reputed to have acquired the manor of Littlecote in Wiltshire as payment for acquitting the owner, William Darell, after a sensational murder trial!

At **Staplehay**, on the way from Wellington to Taunton, is another good hostelry which will welcome you. THE CROWN is popular with locals and visitors alike.

Taunton is a curious mix of county town, shopping centre, education and industrial community. It is ever changing but nothing will ever spoil the skyline. Some of Somerset's best churches are here and their steeples and towers rise with charm and dignity above the buildings of the town. It is old and prosperous and its antiquity has learnt to live in harmony with this latter part of the 20th century. Bath Place always beckons me when I am in Taunton. It is a tranquil Georgian walkway just off the busy High Street. You will find all sorts of shops here but my favourite is MAKERS, owned and run by twelve leading craftwork-shops in Somerset. Everything it sells is hand made: exquisite jewellery and silverwork, delightfully painted silk scarves, tops and ties and lots of useful pots. Ceramic sculpture, wood turnery, baskets, etchings, designer knitwear, furniture and cards make up the remainder of the beautifully made items. They are open Monday to Saturday from 9am-5pm.

Between Taunton and Wellington, SHEPPEYS FARMHOUSE CIDER, Three Bridges, **Bradford-on-Tone**, makes an interesting outing. They are makers of high quality farmhouse cider on a 370 acre farm. You can see the cider making equipment, explore the excellent Farm/Cider Museum or just wander through 30 acres of delightful orchards. If you want to picnic there are special areas in the orchards, and finally, before departing, you can visit the shop which not only sells cider but cheeses and cream as well as other farm produce. The opening hours are Monday to Saturday 8.30am-6pm (7pm in summer). On Sundays from 12-2pm only. Their season starts at Easter and runs through to Christmas. In the winter, only the farm shop is open.

Cider making has been associated with the West Country for centuries and is much a tradition as a craft. Somerset is deep in the heart of the true cider-producing area and no visit to the County is complete without learning a little about this ancient drink. At one time, many *farms produced their own cider, not only to appear on the farm-house table with most meals, but also as an integral part of the farm labourer's wages. Indeed, it was not uncommon for a good worker to drink one or two gallons daily during the long hours of haymaking and harvest time!*

Good cider is made from apples grown especially for this purpose with names like Kingston Black, Stoke Red, Dabinett and Yarlington Mill – evocative of the days when the apples were picked up from under the standard trees by local women for a few pence a sack. These days are gone, however. Todays orchard is likely to be the more intensive bush type, though some good standards remain, where the fruit is harvested by one of the mechanical pickers available. These machines vary from the sophisticated, tractor mounted type, conveying the fruit from ground to trailer, to the less expensive hand operated machines picking up into baskets. Picking usually begins in October.

Withies drying at East Lyng, Sedgemoor

There are still some farmer/cider makers among the small producers, where one is able to obtain a more traditional type of cider as we have seen at Sheppeys. If you are visiting in the Autumn, you may be able to see the milling of the apples, and the pressing out of the pulp, usually by hydraulic press. The juice is fermented out in oak barrels or vats, and after 'racking off' from the sediment or lees, is usually matured in these for some months before being sold.

We have all heard of 'Scrumpy' but this is not really a cider makers term at all. It is generally used to describe a rough, unfiltered cider.

I like **Hatch Beauchamp** where the 450 year old church has some wonderful bench ends, and under a memorial window lies a man who won one of the earliest VCs. As Lieutenant Chard, he was awarded the cross for his gallantry at Rorke's Drift against the Zulus. His leadership had given the willpower to 100 men of the South Wales Borderers to withstand the onslaught of 3000 Zulus for 12 hours suffering less than 30 casualties.

Further up the M5 towards Bridgwater an exit will take you to **East Lyng** and the pretty ROSE & CROWN where the hospitality is second to none. The A361 from there takes you northwards towards the Polden Hills and some beautiful countryside which will tempt you to leave your car and walk. If this does not appeal, take the A372 and make your way to Bridgwater going through **Weston Zoyland**, which originally attracted me because of its odd name but now draws me back because of its history. The ancient church was so much a part of the ghastly night after the battle of Sedgemoor when Monmouth's rebels met their end. Looking at the beauty and peace of the 15th-century roofs with their traceried beams, rich pendants and lovely bosses, it is hard to imagine the awful scene of suffering when 500 of Monmouth's men were locked up in here, badly wounded. They would have lain on the 15th-century benches, crying in despair whilst their fitter comrades were forced to build gibbets outside for the hangings that took place in the morning.

In a chest, the church has a register with an entry describing the battle and another tells how much money the church spent on frankincense to rid it of the awful stench of death. You can read how the bells rang out when Monmouth was captured and for King James II when he rode from Bristol to see the battlefield.

I hope this will not put you off your food because in **Bridgwater** there are two fine hostelries, THE WHITE LION in Bridgwater itself, and THE HARVEST MOON at **North Newton**. It is a memorable town, standing on the River Parret, notable for its Bore, which comes up twice a day with the tidal waters. It once had a castle but there is not much left today. Bridgwater is rich in history and well worth spending time digging it out.

I would hope that you would take time to visit FYNE COURT at **Broomfield**, just 6 miles south of Bridgwater. It is part of the Somerset Trust for Nature Conservation. The Nature Reserve has trails, guided walks, a countryside information centre and a shop, and is open daily.

Admission is free and car parking costs a mere 40p. Special Interest Days are held here providing an opportunity for everyone to pursue their Natural History interests in a non-academic atmosphere. The interesting and enthusiastic approach of the study day leaders, who are all experts in their fields, ensures a fascinating and enjoyable day. To obtain further information ring (0823) 451587

Perhaps you may care to stop at **East Huntspill** and sample the hospitality of THE BASONBRIDGE INN, before making your way to NEW ROAD FARM. Family run, it demonstrates both modern and traditional methods of farming. Over 60 different breeds of animals can be found here, and visitors are encouraged to enjoy the complete freedom of Derek and Pauline Kidner's home.

Somerset County Council's Levels Visitor Centre, which offers unusual audio visual effects and 'hands on' experiences for all ages, is part of your visit to the farm. There are children's areas around the farm and there is freedom to explore and make contact with the animals. There is something to see and something to experience both indoors and out throughout the season: a blacksmith at work, feeding routines, hay-making, sheepshearing, incubation techniques. New Road opens every day from Easter to the end of September. Weekends only in the winter. It is as well to telephone for details of the opening times. The number is (0278) 783250.

From the joy of the countryside to the fun of the seaside. **Highbridge**, with THE WHITE HART in which you can get good pub food, is only a little way from **Burnham-on-Sea** and from there the coast leads on to **Berrow** and **Brean**. A wonderful stretch of sand with all sorts of things for everyone. Before I tell you about what you can do and see just let me remind you that in Berrow there is a super restaurant THE YEW TREE which you should not miss.

Burnham-on-Sea does not have much of its medieval past remaining. The church still stands even if it does look a little unsafe with its west tower decidedly leaning. I enjoy the walk that one can take along the Esplanade and the riverside as far as the old docks at Highbridge. It is almost derelict now even though until 1948 the port at Highbridge remained working. If you are a golf enthusiast you will enjoy the super championship 18 hole course. It is right by the sea. The little town also has a very good indoor swimming pool.

Berrow is popular as a camping and caravanning area, not surprising with its easy access to the beach. If you are not of the bucket and spade brigade you may well enjoy THE ANIMAL FARM COUNTRY PARK and LAND OF LEGENDS in Red Road, Berrow.

There are all kinds of rare breeds, domestic farm animals and even a few surprises! You have the opportunity to feed and make friends with many of the animals. The static display of machinery and tools of yesteryear will take you back in time to when the horses were the power on the land. At various points round the park information is displayed which provides detailed material relating to the animals, local wildlife and conservation. The Land of Legends recreates scenes of the folklore of the West Country. It is quite spellbinding and the stories seem to enchant adults as much as the children. Animal Farm is open from Easter until the end of October from 10-5pm every day.

Brean Down Tropical Bird Garden

Along the seven miles of golden sands between Burnham and Brean there are endless things and sights to delight your eyes. At the very end, a great hump which was once described to me as a submerging hippo, projects three-quarters of a mile into the sea. Man has probably lived here since the end of the Ice Age 10,000 years ago. There are Bronze Age barrows and burial cairns, an Iron Age fort, Celtic field systems and on the second highest point of Brean Down, the foundations of a Roman temple. This small area provides hours of pleasure and the vegetation of the western-facing slope is almost unique in Britain. Nor must one forget the BREAN DOWN TROPICAL BIRD GARDEN.

Close by this natural paradise is the lively BREAN LEISURE PARK which offers constant fun and entertainment. It has over 30 *attractions for all the family including The Farmers Tavern: one of Somerset's leading nightspots and is open all the year round, offering live cabaret, dining and dancing. It is so busy that it is advisable to book a table particularly if you want to enjoy Sunday lunch here. The Farmers Den provides a family room facility and in the main season family entertainment is presented at which children are welcome.*

The Barn and Bar-B-Q is another family entertainment venue adjoining the fun park. If you would like to stay at Brean Leisure Park you can hire one of their luxury holiday homes, or book a pitch for your tent, tourer or motor home. The Seaside Fun Park is open from 11am-dusk, Saturdays and Sundays, from Easter until October 1st, and also daily from May 25th until the end of the first week in September. The Farmers Tavern is open all year round. The Farmers Den: nightly from May 25th until the end of September from 7.30pm-11pm. The Swimming Pool with Aquaslides: weekends from Easter and daily from 10am-6pm from May 19th-until September 29th. Finally, the 18 hole golf course is open all the year and visitors are welcomed Monday to Friday.

*If you would rather opt for something a little quieter I would suggest lunch at THE WHEATSHEAF INN at **Chapel Allerton**, and afterwards visit ASHTON WINDMILL. This unique 18th-century flour mill stands on the 'Isle' of Wedmore, a ridge giving commanding views of the Cheddar Gorge, Somerset Levels and Brent Knoll, and is the only complete mill left in Somerset. Mention is made of a mill on this elevated site as far back as 1317. A straight sided construction, the windmill is girded by 3 iron hoops, which were added by the last miller, John Stevens, to ensure that the sails ran true.*

Restored to working condition in 1958, with renovations carried out in 1979 by the Dorothea Restoration Engineers, it is now maintained by volunteers under the guidance of Sedgemoor District Council. Open 2.30-4.30pm every Sunday and Bank Holiday from Easter till the end of September. Admission is free, but naturally donations are appreciated.

BASON BRIDGE INN

Public House

East Huntspill
Highbridge, Somerset
Tel: (0278) 782616

East Huntspill lies peacefully on the fringes of Sedgemoor between the Mendips and the Quantocks, and it is here that you will find The Bason Bridge Inn. It is hard to imagine that this magical haven for wild birds was the setting, in 1685, for one of Englands' most historical events, the Battle of Sedgemoor.

This charming pub is about 100 years old, and manages to capture the heart of every visitor with its warm and friendly atmosphere. Apart from the bar, there is a function room which caters for up to 75 people, making it the ideal venue for small weddings or other private parties. One of the main attractions to the Bason Bridge, is the Double skittle alley that will bring hours of enjoyment for the whole family.

Food is freshly prepared using local, seasonal produce. A variety of homemade dishes are available and change daily. Choose from the specials, dish of the day or enjoy a quick snack of beautifully presented sandwiches or a crusty filled roll. Vegetarians are not forgotten and imaginative dishes have been conjured up to suit every palette. The menu is carefully assembled to ensure everyone is accomodated for.

USEFUL INFORMATION

OPEN: M-T:11.30-2.30pm, 7-11pm
F-S: 11.30-3pm, 6.30-11pm, Sun:
12-3pm, 7-10.30pm
CHILDREN: Yes, childrens room.
Double skittle alley.
CREDIT CARDS: None.
LICENSED: Full licence.
GARDEN: Large garden.

RESTAURANT: Home cooking.
BAR FOOD: Yes, specials, steaks,
sandwiches, rolls & Seasonal
produce.
VEGETARIAN: Yes.
ACCESS FOR THE DISABLED:
Level entrance.

29 High Street,
Bridgwater, Somerset

Tel: (0278) 429506

THE WHITE LION
Public House

This is a lively attractive pub right in the town centre of Bridgwater. It has been a hostelry for the last century during which time it has collected within its four walls a great deal of atmosphere and is obviously very popular with local people. It has original low beams and stone walls and as you walk in you are enveloped in a warm and friendly circle. An almost L shaped bar leads up to a slightly raised section which is used for darts and children can also use this part set back from the bar.

From the old photographs which hang on the walls you can piece together some of the pubs interesting history, and if this fascinates you the sociable landlady, Mrs Jones is always willing to spare the time to tell you more. Bridgwater has a great deal of history and The White Lion has certainly had something to offer to it through the years as it still does today. It is an excellent place for the visitor to take time out from sightseeing or for business people to pop in for a quick sustaining lunch and at extremely reasonable prices.

On the menu you will find good quality, no nonsense fare served in generous portions. Jacket Potatoes with an imaginative number of fillings and a first class Chilli Con Carni are among the favourite dishes which also includes a particularly good sweet and sour chicken. If you do not want something hot then a plentiful Ploughmans with crisp bread is tempting as are the freshly made, well filled sandwiches.

USEFUL INFORMATION

OPEN: 10.30am-11pm Food: 12-2pm
CHILDREN: Yes. No special facilities
CREDIT CARDS: None taken
LICENSED: Full Licence.
GARDEN: No

RESTAURANT: Not applicable
BAR FOOD: Good, wholesome food
VEGETARIAN: By request
ACCESS FOR THE DISABLED:
   Level entrance

THE WHEATSHEAF INN

Inn

Chapel Allerton,
Nr. Axbridge, Somerset
Tel: (0934) 712494

It is a great pleasure to come across a true country pub which is easily accessible from Bristol, Weston Super Mare and other seaside places like Burnham on Sea. The Wheatsheaf is set in a charming rural area and is one of those places in which one feels instantly at ease. Ian and Joan Wigginton, the landlords, are without doubt a very large ingredient in the friendliness of this establishment. They have worked very hard to make the Wheatsheaf what it is today.

Inside there are two comfortable bars with a very small restaurant area at one end. In winter there are roaring fires in both bars. The pub has its devoted regulars and, if you are lucky, you may be invited to join them for a game of darts or skittles. Watch out though, they are skilled and very competitive. The pub teams play regularly against other sides during the winter months.

In summer, the large garden leading from a verandah, on which hang an abundance of flowering baskets, is an ideal spot to sit at one of the rustic tables and enjoy either a drink or a meal. Amongst the many dishes on the menu there is almost always fresh salmon, perfectly cooked and served with crisp salads. In the winter, Joan, who deals with the catering, makes her own special steak and kidney pies and they are justly renowned. The Wheatsheaf also has a name for serving the most tender, succulent, rare beef. Of course there are specials every day and all the usual food one would expect on a good bar menu. If you are a vegetarian you will be delighted to find a delicious Butter bean bake.

USEFUL INFORMATION

OPEN: 11.30-2.30pm 6.30-11pm
(Food – last orders 9.30pm)
CHILDREN: Well behaved very
welcome
CREDIT CARDS: Not applicable
LICENSED: Full licence
GARDEN: Very nice large garden
with tables.

RESTAURANT: Traditional English
Fare
BAR FOOD: Wide range delicious
food
VEGETARIAN: 3 dishes usually
ACCESS FOR THE DISABLED: One
small step

THE ROSE AND CROWN
Free House

East Lyng,
Taunton, Somerset.
Tel: (0823) 69235

This charming pub just outside Taunton, on the A361 Taunton/Glastonbury Road, is so well liked that the Proprietors, Pete Thyer and Derek Mason can almost tell the day of the week it is by a visit from their regular clientele who travel quite a distance to sample the hospitality. It is not the place for anyone who wants juke boxes, fruit machines or Pool tables. For those who like to enjoy a good meal in comfortable surroundings and a splendid atmosphere it would be difficult to find somewhere better.

Pete has been in the business for years but Derek is a comparative newcomer having given up the sea in favour of this convivial life style. They are super hosts and not only do you receive a warm welcome but they ensure the farewell is equally friendly. This is one of the reasons why so many people put The Rose and Crown high on their list of favourite places to visit. On balmy summer days the lovely, well laid out garden is an added bonus especially as guests can dine outside.

You have the choice of eating by reservation in the Restaurant or electing to have a Bar Meal which can be eaten in the Bar or in the little Dining Room where children are welcome. The Restaurant has its own excellent menu whilst the Bar has a wide choice including succulent steaks, daily Blackboard specials and the lightest of omelettes. If you have a sweet tooth you will revel in the choice of Home-made sweets. Food is available throughout the week and on Sundays Roast Beef with all the trimmings is extremely popular; make sure you book for this.

USEFUL INFORMATION

OPEN: Mon-Sat: 11-2.30pm, 6.30-11pm, Sun: 12-3.00pm, 7-10.30pm
CHILDREN: Welcome in Dining Room
CREDIT CARDS: Access/Visa/Mastercard
LICENSED: Full Licence
GARDEN: Lovely garden with tables

RESTAURANT: Steaks a speciality. Reservations please.
BAR FOOD: Wide choice. Daily Specials
VEGETARIAN: Dishes available daily.
ACCESS FOR THE DISABLED: Easy access. Welcome

THE WHITE HART
Public House

100, Church Street,
Highbridge, Somerset
Tel: (0278) 783520

Highbridge lies on the A 38 between Bridgwater and Weston-Super-Mare, two miles from the spacious beaches of Burnham on Sea. In the middle of Church Street there is a friendly, comfortable pub, The White Hart, which has plenty of parking space.

Paul and Gaynor Howitt are the landlords here. They have made themselves very popular in the years that they have been in residence, and attracted a clientele who come regularly for the well kept traditional ale, the food, and the fun that is generated. No newcomer to their midst is allowed to feel a stranger for much longer than it takes to get a drink in your hand. You can try your hand at Pool, Darts or try knocking the pins over in the Skittle Alley. The bar talk covers all sorts of subjects, but if you happen to be there in the autumn, it will probably be about the advent of the Bridgwater Carnival, which started as a Goose Fair in the 11th century and is held every November; the biggest free show in Europe.

The food is simple, home-cooked and plentiful. It varies from daily specials to succulent steaks. You will find a range of freshly cut sandwiches starting from 80p, a good variety of Ploughmans lunches, special childrens portions, and vegetarian dishes too. The staff are friendly and helpful and the whole atmosphere is that of a good family pub.

USEFUL INFORMATION

OPEN: Food: 11-2.30pm. Mon-Fri:
11-4pm, Sun: 12-2pm
CHILDREN: Welcome
CREDIT CARDS: None taken
LICENSED: Full Licence
GARDEN: Enclosed garden rear of
pub

RESTAURANT: Not applicable
BAR FOOD: Wide variety, good
value
VEGETARIAN: On request
ACCESS FOR THE DISABLED:
Level entrance

Hillcommon,
Nr. Taunton, Somerset

Tel: (0823) 400279

BARON OF BEEF
Restaurant/Carvery

The Baron of Beef at Hillcommon is the most welcoming place. Nothing is too much trouble and their motto is to try to please almost all of the people almost all of the time. It would be a complete ingrate who did not appreciate anything they have to offer.

You choose your first course from the large selection on the buffet table. When you have finished you are asked to make your way to the Carving area where the Chef will serve you with meats carved from the joints on offer. After which you help yourself from the selection of hot vegetables. The pleasant staff take orders for wine, drinks, sweet and coffee. It is an excellent meal at a very fair price. In the constant pursuit of pleasing everyone there is a separate menu for Vegetarians and another for the Fish lover and if this is not good enough then a succulent Steak or Roast Chicken is available. Simple meals are available too. Light, fluffy omelettes with various fillings or sustaining Ploughman's lunches. Pizzas perhaps or a tasty cottage pie. The Carvery is available Tuesday to Saturday and for Sunday Lunch. An enjoyable place for a family occasion.

USEFUL INFORMATION

OPEN: Tues-Sat: 12-2.00pm, 7-9.30pm, Sun: 12-2.00pm
CHILDREN: Yes. Half price
CREDIT CARDS: Access/Visa
LICENSED: Full Licence
GARDEN: No. 40 Car parking spaces.

RESTAURANT: Carvery. Home cooking.
BAR FOOD: Not applicable
VEGETARIAN: Special Menu
ACCESS FOR THE DISABLED: Yes

THE HARVEST MOON

Public House

Church Road, North Newton,
Bridgwater, Somerset

Tel: (0278) 662570

It is quite unusual for a comparatively new pub to acquire a really good atmosphere but the 30 year old Harvest Moon has done just that. No doubt much of it is down to the friendly couple, Sue and Tony Hughes, who are mine hosts, aided and abetted by their welcoming staff. It is located in the pretty village of North Newton and easily reached from Junction 24 of the M5. You turn towards Taunton into North Petherton and turn left by the playing fields. The pub is situated in the centre of the village opposite the junior school.

Lively and interesting personalities frequent the Harvest Moon most of whom were born and bred in the village which all helps to make this a very good place to lunch or indeed visit at anytime. It is surrounded by open countryside with many attractive walks around the village and along the Bridgwater to Taunton Canal towpath. Maunsel House is nearby, a perfect place to spend an afternoon after visiting the pub.

The food here is all home made and delicious. Steaks could possibly be called the speciality of the house but amongst the varied menu are such dishes as Beef, Walnut and Guinness Pie, Chicken and Mushroom Bake, Nutty Vegetable Crumble and if you only have time for a snack what about trying a Sausage and Apple Burger or locally made Duck Sausages? On Sundays you can indulge in a plentiful traditional roast meal which includes a choice of sweet as well as starter. There are always fresh vegetables and the roast is changed each week. This is a really good value for money food pub.

USEFUL INFORMATION

OPEN: Food 12-2.00pm,7-10.00pm
  except Mondays
CHILDREN: Welcome in restaurant
  & skittle alley
CREDIT CARDS: None taken
LICENSED: Full Licence. Wine list.
GARDEN: In summer tables outside

RESTAURANT: Home cooked food
BAR FOOD: Good variety. Home
  cooked.
VEGETARIAN: 2 dishes on menu
ACCESS FOR THE DISABLED: No
  level entrance

Honiton Road, Staplehay,
Taunton, Somerset

Tel: (0823) 272560

THE CROWN INN

Public House

Taking the old Honiton Road, B1370, out of Taunton towards Blagdon Hill and you will see a turning off to your right for Staplehay, a quiet village with many country walks close to hand. In the centre is The Crown Inn, built at the turn of the century, it is charming, warm and friendly. Just the place to enjoy a good lunch.

Chris Shaw and Christine Bevan have recently taken over The Crown and created not only the nice atmosphere but a super restaurant as well. The menu has been designed to produce home cooked food using as much local produce as possible, and there is no doubt that the excellent dishes are building a reputation for the Crown very quickly. The prices are reasonable too. Add to that Chris Shaw's skillful handling of the beer and you cannot go far wrong.

Everyday the menu has a variety of dishes. Guinness and Steak Pie is a speciality. The home made soups are full of flavour and sustenance. Boeuf Bourgignon is one of the regulars favourites. Vegetarians are catered for to order. On Sundays there is a traditional roast with all the trimmings which may be beef, turkey or pork. Bar snacks are always available apart from Sunday lunchtime.

USEFUL INFORMATION

OPEN: Weekdays 11.30am.-11.00pm
CHILDREN: Yes.
CREDIT CARDS: No
LICENSED: Full Licence
GARDEN: No. Car parking available

RESTAURANT: Home cooked fayre
BAR FOOD: Snacks in addition to
above. (Not Sunday mid-day)
VEGETARIAN: As requested
ACCESS FOR THE DISABLED: Yes

*A bridge over the Moat leads into the magic of the walled
Formal Garden at Barrington Court.*

INCLUDES:

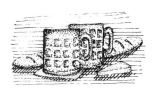

*"**Snails:** I find this a somewhat disturbing dish, but the sauce is divine. What I do is order escargots, and tell them to 'hold' the snails."*

Miss Piggy

SOUTH SOMERSET

One leaflet I read said 'Come and share the secrets of South Somerset with us'. I did, and this is what I want to pass on to you. It is a part of the county that has just about everything. To the west the Levels and Moors, to the south the Hamstone country and to the east the mystical Camelot country. It is fabulous; filled with beauty, dignified monuments, stately homes and for those who love walking it is wonderful.

There are three small towns to which I have become attached over the years. **Langport**, a town of narrow streets and full of antique shops, lies on the River Parrett. The old warehouses standing by the riverside bear witness to the time when the town was busy with waterborne trade coming from Wales via Bridgwater. It was once a walled town but all that remains of the Wall is THE HANGING CHAPEL – built over what was the East gate. I used to think it had something to do with Judge Jeffreys but for once he is not responsible. Langport did play a decisive part in the Civil War though, in 1645 an important battle was fought on its outskirts, the site of which can still be seen if you follow the B3155 to Somerton. You will find a side road leading to **Wagg** and **Huish Episcopi** with the small waterway of the Wagg Rhyne alongside. The Royalists were well positioned on the Langport side where there was a very narrow ford across the rhyne. Only four horsemen could cross it abreast, but Fairfax ordered his cavalry to charge and after a fierce battle the day was won. The Royalists were defeated, their morale broken and the end of the Civil War was in sight.

Go on to Huish Episcopi to see the historic church of St Marys with its wonderful Perpendicular tower, niches and pinnacles. It is open in daylight hours. Afterwards go across to ELI'S or to use its proper name the ROSE AND CROWN, a truly traditional inn. Its nickname comes from the family who have run it for 120 years. Two or three miles to the east is **Long Sutton** with an excellent pub, THE LIME KILN. What an opportunity to have a good lunch and then take a look at the old Court House which has delightful windows, as do many buildings here. The 15th-century church must be seen for so many reasons, not the least the fantastic 450 year old pulpit with a 17th-century canopy. It rests on a base carved in tiers, rising from a slender, panelled pillar.

Somerton claims to be the capital of ancient Wessex, and justifiably boasts much to entrance one for hours. The Church of St Michael has a roof that was created by the monks of Mulcheney from 7,000 fetter pieces. These monks obviously had a sense of humour: incorporated in the roof is a beer barrel playing on the name of Abbot Bere!. If you wander *down the leafy lane beside the church you will come into a delightful square of Georgian buildings, which has the misnomer of 'Cow Square', leading you into Broad Street which once was called Pig Lane. There has to be a reason for these names but I have found none. Somerton is graced with several good hostelries including THE RED LION which is still licensed to hire out post horses, and THE WHITE HART which stands on the site of Somerton's ancient castle.*

The Market Cross, Somerton

*Parking in **Martock** is free – what a blessing. It is such a pretty, dignified little town with houses built in the local golden hamstone. The superb church of All Saints is the second largest in Somerset and you will drool over its wonderful roof. It is a popular spot for bird watchers because of its proximity to what is known as Wet Moor which in summer attracts curlews and redshanks.*

*I started out exploring one day, having had a good lunch at THE ROYAL OAK, **Stoke-St-Gregory**. Whilst I was there the landlord had been good enough to suggest several places which were within easy reach. In Stoke-St-Gregory there are two traditional Somerset basket and hurdle makers. At THE WILLOW & WETLAND VISITOR CENTRE not only can you view the process but there is also an extensive wetlands exhibition which reveals the unique landscape of the Somerset Levels. Add to this a Basket Museum and you will have a good reason for visiting. Open: Monday to Friday 9am-5pm with guided tours from*

10am-4pm at half hourly intervals. On Saturdays the times change to 10-5pm with just the showroom and the shop being open. Then there is THE ENGLISH BASKET CENTRE where not only can you see baskets and hurdles being made but you can walk through the adjoining growing willow beds. They are open from Monday-Friday 8am-5pm and on Saturday from 9am-1pm.

My next stop was **Curry Rivel** *where the lovely 15th-century church looks over the village green. Take a look at the stone figures adorning the walls. There is one above the porch playing the bagpipes and round the corner another playing the violin – they are known locally as the 'hunky punks'!*

MULCHENEY ABBEY is close by which was founded by the Benedictines in AD950. Standing in beautiful grounds, you can see the excavated ground plan of the abbey church, preserved remains of the south cloister and the abbot's lodgings. It is open from Good Friday – 30th September daily from 10am-6pm. Also, in the village opposite the church, is the Priest's House, a thatched stone cottage built by the monks in 1308 to house the vicar of the parish. Although much has been altered inside, the exterior still displays a Gothic doorway, mullioned windows and the superb two-tiered window to the hall, with trefoil heads to the upper lights.

Just one mile south, the potter, John Leach, works from his thatched workshop. A selection of unique handthrown pots, including signed individual pieces is always available in the Pottery shop. Open Monday to Friday 9-5pm and Saturdays 9-1pm.

A place of peaceful delight is EAST LAMBROOK MANOR GARDEN near **South Petherton**. *It is an all year garden created by the late Margery Fish and made famous through her many books. It is both a traditional cottage style garden and an important collection of plants. The informality of this Grade I listed garden creates a tremendous sense of tranquillity. Almost in the centre of the 2 acre garden is a 17th-century Malthouse which houses plant lists and photographs of the development of the garden since 1938. Open Monday to Saturday from 10am-5pm and Bank Holiday Weekends. It is closed from November 1st – January 15th. No dogs are allowed and it is unsuitable for wheelchairs.*

Had I chosen to go south after leaving Stoke-St-Gregory I might well have ended up at THE WHITE HART INN at **Corfe** *– nothing to do with Corfe Castle in Dorset but a pretty little village in its own right. The route is delightful, running through winding lanes. The villages are small and picturesque with some of the most beautiful churches in the country. WIDCOMBE BIRD GARDENS sit tucked away near here. A* *super place to visit. The 10 acres of mature parkland contain many rare trees and shrubs, a large lake and ponds which are the habitat of flamingoes, geese, swans and other waterfowl. The walled garden area is the home of Macaws, Cockatoos, Amazon Parrots and one of the finest collections of Brushed Tongued Parrots in the West Country. Open daily 10.30-5.30pm from April to October. Free Car and Coach Park but no dogs please.*

On to **Wadeford** *where another hostelry,* THE HAYMAKER INN, *is more than worth a visit. The road will lead you to* **Chard**, *the highest town in Somerset. The Romans gave it its straight street, the Saxons its name but Nature gave it something very different. A stream runs down each side of the main street, dividing at the bottom where one half sallies forth to pour itself into the English Channel, the other goes north to enter the Bristol Channel. It has always seemed to me that Nature is telling us something. A little stream divides, gets stronger and meets again as part of the mighty Atlantic Ocean.*

Fire destroyed much of Chard in 1577 but the perfectly proportioned 15th-century church survived as well as the Court House where Judge Jeffreys held trial after the Monmouth Rebellion. My favourite building is CHOUGH'S HOTEL *built in 1644. A building of mystery and intrigue. Judge Jeffreys stayed there. You can still see his coat of arms in his bedroom. It is a hotel of hidden bedrooms, sealed cellars and what may have been an escape tunnel for priests fleeing from persecution. You will find a mummified bird kept in a coffin and superstition says it must always remain. Having taken all this in I suggest you go to* THE BELL AND CROWN, *just off the main street, for some refreshment. From here you could set off for* FORDE ABBEY *founded by Cistercian monks 900 years ago. It remains a family home unaltered since the mid 17th century. 30 acres of gardens surround the house, with herbaceous borders, magnificent trees, shrubs and an outstanding Bog garden. The Gardens are open daily throughout the year from 10am-4.30pm. The Abbey is open from Easter until the end of October, Sundays, Wednesdays and Bank Holidays 1pm-4.30pm*

Two miles north of Chard is HORNSBURY MILL *where the water mill still works. It is such a pleasant place to be. You can have the most extravagant cream tea, lunch or dine, or even stay in en-suite bed and breakfast accommodation.*

Cricket St Thomas *is midway between Chard and Crewkerne. It has one of the best Wildlife and Leisure Parks in the country. The Manor House was used for the TV series 'To the Manor Born' which many of us have enjoyed – even the repeats! It is set in a valley of* *outstanding natural beauty and provides a wonderful place for a happy family day out or as a member of an organised party. It is a working estate covering over a thousand acres. You can see anything from Asian elephants taking their daily walk to performing Sealions disporting themselves. The Heavy Horse Centre is one of the few places in the country where these gentle giants are still bred and cared for. The miniature railway winds its way along the far side of the valley crossing a 40ft high bridge over the lake at one point. The Adventure Playground features a life-sized American fort, in addition to a large variety of 'assault course' challenges set along the woodland paths. Go there; it is excellent.*

Penguins at Cricket St. Thomas

One tends to forget FERNE ANIMAL SANCTUARY, just three miles from Chard in the other direction. It started in 1939 when so many animals became homeless because their owners went off to war. The work of the sanctuary, which is a charity, continues today and they have some two hundred animals from horse to hamsters.

*WINDWHISTLE HILL beckons all who see it with its wonderful avenue of beech trees. Climb it and, on a clear day, you will be rewarded with a view of the Bristol Channel on one side and the English Channel on the other, but always there is the enchanting sight of gentle Somerset beneath you. You will look down on **Crewkerne** from here. A town whose streets all converge on the market square. It has many old stone houses* *and four groups of almshouses but the church is the magnet. It is a grand 15th-century cruciform church with glorious windows. The west front is almost cathedral like. Inside it is a little disappointing but the width of the windows brings light to the lovely panelled roofs. Thirteen great stone angels stand holding up the enchanting nave roof. Having drunk in all this beauty may I suggest a little drive down the road to* **North Perrott***, where THE MANOR ARMS will refresh the inner man.*

One of the West Country's most delightful and interesting formal and woodland gardens of over 10 acres, CLAPTON COURT is just south of Crewkerne. With formal terraces, a recently designed rose garden, spacious lawns, mixed borders and the largest Ash tree in Great Britain, it is a garden for all seasons, from the dazzling display of bulbs to the autumn colours. Many rare and unusual plants are for sale, also, fuchsias and pelargoniums. Open March to October, Mondays to Fridays 10.30am-5pm and Sundays from 2-5pm. Licenced restaurant. Dogs not allowed.

Shepton Beauchamp *does not boast a VC like Hatch Beauchamp but it has a wonderful 15th-century church, with a tower that is splendid inside and out, and not far away is a pub that is worthy of its name THE DUKE OF YORK. It is a happy place in which to drink or eat.*

Many people drive straight through **South Petherton** *which is a pity because it contains a unique enterprise known as 'Global Village' which imports Village Art from more than 30 countries including many of the Third World. The items are almost too numerous to mention – wrought iron, silver, jewellery, carvings, 'wobbly ducks' from Thailand which quack and wag their tails!. Global Village has its headquarters here in a disused chapel, and there are two shops open to the public. It supplies many stores in the U.K., including Harrods, and exports world wide. It is an experience not to be missed. South Petherton has a fine church, the second highest octagonal tower in the country. Today it houses the effigy of a curly headed knight dressed in chain mail. He is Sir Philip de Albini who died in 1292 but he was not buried with ceremony. His remains were unearthed by the side of the road where a pit was being dug for a petrol tank! If you were a NatWest customer in South Petherton you would constantly be reminded of the Monmouth rebellion; opposite the bank is Market House where three men were hanged in the courtyard from a beam by the order of the dreaded Judge Jeffreys.*

From here it would be sacrilegious not to traverse the narrow lanes to **Barrington***. It is a typical off the beaten track South Somerset village which will make you want to explore others like* **Hinton St George,**

Chiselborough, Norton-sub-Hamdon and *West Chinnock*. *It has thatched hamstone cottages, a lovely 13th-century church and a good pub, THE ROYAL OAK, in which the walls of the bar are hung with relics of horse plough days, and, nearby, the delight of BARRINGTON COURT.*

Barrington Court

Ever since **Ilminster** *has been by-passed it has become a pleasure to enter the town. You will not be able to miss the church tower which is almost out of place in a small town. It was copied about 550 years ago from the central tower of Wells Cathedral. It stands in all its glory with 24 pierced stone windows to let out the sound of the bells, 22 pinnacles at the top and above all, the cap of a stair turret with 16 gargoyles and 32 canopies. Preferably, do not go inside because you will feel a sense of being let down after what you have seen. It was largely rebuilt in the 19th century and it has been spoiled. What will not disappoint you is THE LORD NELSON where you will receive a friendly hospitable welcome. Ilminster has PERRY'S CIDER MILLS at Dawlish Wake, a Cider farm that specialises in high quality farmhouse cider. You are encouraged to taste before buying. Beware it is very potent! Open all year, weekdays 9am-5.30pm. Saturdays 9.30am-4.30pm, Sundays 9.30am-1pm only.*

If you want to visit either THE FLEET AIR ARM MUSEUM, WORLDWIDE BUTTERFLIES and LULLINGSTONE SILK FARM at Compton House, or THE HAYNES SPARKFORD MOTOR MUSEUM, you will be able to find yourself some good places to eat in **Yeovil.** *There is THE PLUCKNETT HOTEL, THE RED HOUSE INN or the simple RAILWAY INN HOTEL. Further to the west is the very nice hotel THE FOUR ACRES at* **West Coker** *which would be an ideal base either before or after taking a look at the remarkable church which has a font that is well over 700 years old. It also has a rarity, or had when I was last there, two windows in the turret of the tower still glazed with horn as in medieval days.*

Getting back to The Fleet Air Arm Museum, it is a memorable introduction to the Fleet Air Arm – the men, women and aircraft who provide the Royal Navy with its air power. To help you enjoy the breathtaking exhibits more simply, the Museum is divided into sections and each display takes a piece of the Fleet Air Arm's history bringing it alive for you and your family. With over 50 historic aircraft on display and 5 major new attractions, there is plenty to appeal to all ages. Open daily including weekends except Christmas Eve, Christmas Day and Boxing Day, from 10am-5.30pm March-October and 10am-4.30pm November to February.

Travelling along the dual carriageway from Yeovil towards Sherborne will bring you to the Worldwide Butterflies and Lullingstone Silk Farm at Compton House. In the setting of the house and its grounds visitors can see butterflies alive and flying in exotic surroundings. You will see some wonderful displays and you will be encouraged to learn to conserve. Worldwide Butterflies was founded by Robert Goodden over thirty years ago, creating a public awareness of butterflies that has spread enormously. The Lullingstone Silk Farm has supplied unique English silk for the last two coronations, for the Queen's wedding dress, and for many other royal occasions including the wedding of the Prince and Princess of Wales. Here you can learn the ancient history of silk and see the silkworms producing English silk from the egg to the finished skein of soft, gleaming yarn. Open 10am-5pm daily from April 1st to 30th October (Good Friday if earlier). If you want a cup of coffee or tea and one of the largest cream cakes you have ever seen pop into the LITTLE MOTOCHEF almost next door. It is one of the most spotless places I have ever visited.

THE HAYNES SPARKFORD MOTOR MUSEUM enthrals most people. You can look over the unique range of over 200 Veteran, Vintage and Classic cars, motorcycles, racing cars and bikes. All in as original and as new condition as possible. Open 9.30am-5.30pm seven days a week. Nearly every car and bike in the Museum is driven at least every six months on the specially constructed 1 kilometre Display and

Demonstration road round the Museum. Something like a 1930 4 litre Bentley or 400S Lamborghini Countach may be circulating when you visit.

Set in glorious countryside, almost in the shadow of Cadbury Castle, the reputed Camelot of King Arthur and his court, the Museum (a Charitable Trust) has an ambience at one with the chivalrous ideals of the gallant King and his Knights of the Round Table. The Pit Stop cafe is open most days but if you would rather picnic than eat indoors you are welcome to do so and enjoy the view of the rolling hills and woodlands.

MONTACUTE HOUSE belonging to the National Trust, should not be omitted whilst you are in this neck of the woods. This stately 16th-century country house with formal gardens set in a landscape park, is a gem. The House is open from 30th March – 3rd November daily 12noon – 5.30pm except Tuesdays. The Garden and Park are open daily throughout the year from 11.30am-5.30pm except Tuesdays.

*I have left **North Cadbury** to last because we are coming into Camelot country. Romantic and wonderful and so full of expectation. It is a charming village of old stone cottages, orchards, lovely walks a wonderful church, a gabled Elizabethan house and if that was not enough, a fine inn, THE CATASH.*

THE BELL AND CROWN
Inn

Coombe Street,
Chard, Somerset
Tel: (0460) 62470

Tucked away behind the main street of Chard is the Bell and Crown. One of its many virtues is the large car park which, in a town where parking is not the easiest thing to do, is a blessing. It is the sort of pub that is popular with the locals who regularly visit the long bar. The atmosphere is pleasantly welcoming with well polished dark oak tables on which stand small vases of freshly picked flowers. Visitors will find the Bell and Crown particularly convenient to have lunch and then take off for a wander around this old market town. Chard is also only 20 minutes from the historic and delightful Lyme Regis, on the Dorset coast, just over the Somerset border.

There is a small beer garden at the rear where you can sit and enjoy a drink on a warm day and also a Skittle Alley in which you can test your skills. You may inveigle one of the locals to have a game with you but watch out – they are experts! Food is very important of course. You will find simple food here, well-cooked and presented and, most importantly, extremely reasonably priced. The daily specials are very popular and in addition there are many pub grub favourites such as Scampi and chips, tender steaks, various chicken dishes and many snack items. The sandwiches are always freshly prepared to order and well filled. The staff are a friendly crowd who offer service with a smile and have no objection to answering questions about the area. Sunday lunches have such a following that it is necessary to book in advance. Roast Beef or Roast Chicken is always on the Sunday menu and is incredible value at £3.50p

USEFUL INFORMATION

OPEN: 11-2.30pm, 7-11.00pm Sun: 12-2.30pm, 7-10.30pm
CHILDREN: Welcome to eat
CREDIT CARDS: None taken
LICENSED: Full licence
GARDEN: Beer Garden. Large car park

RESTAURANT: Not applicable
BAR FOOD: Wide choice home cooked pub food
VEGETARIAN: 1-2 dishes daily
ACCESS FOR THE DISABLED: Yes.

THE WHITE HART INN
Public House

Corfe,
Taunton, Somerset
Tel: (082342) 388

The White Hart is the only pub in the picturesque village of Corfe just three miles south of Taunton on the B 3170 road to Honiton. It is a super place to lunch before going to the racecourse a mile away or for a wander in the beauty of the Blackdown Hills.

In 1566 the building was part of a farm and was converted into a pub about 1751. It really is an attractive and friendly place to which you are welcomed by John and Bev Davey. They can seat 48 people in the quaint eating areas, and if the weather is kind an additional verandah area comes into use. In the bar you will find a roaring fire, exposed stonework and sturdy beams, and there is no piped music which does much to kill conversation.

All the food is freshly prepared by John and Bev with the help of a young chef. From the varied menu you can have a three course meal which might include Helenstowe Sole, a dish unique to the White Hart, or Duck breast grilled and served with a pepper sauce. Traditional 'Door Steps', a selection of fillings stuffed between wedges of granary or white bread make a meal in themselves. Coffee is always available. There is a full menu seven days a week except Sunday lunchtime when the concentration is on the traditional Roast Beef or Chicken followed by a wide selection of desserts.

USEFUL INFORMATION

OPEN: Everyday, Food served: 11.30-2.30pm. 6.30-9.30pm
CHILDREN: Yes. Children's menu
CREDIT CARDS: Visa/Mastercard/ Access/Eurocard
LICENSED: 4 Real Ales. Wines, Non alchoholic & beverages
GARDEN: Patios front & rear, skittle alley, Children welcome

RESTAURANT: International with provincial French influences
BAR FOOD: Trad. Famous 'Doorstep' sandwiches
VEGETARIAN: Yes. 3 dishes
ACCESS FOR THE DISABLED: No

Station Road,
Ilminster, Somerset

Tel: (0460) 52532

THE LORD NELSON
Public House

You will find the Lord Nelson Inn just off the A303 about half a mile towards Ilminster. The Inn began as a cider house known as Slope Inn. When the railway was built the name changed to Railway Hotel and it became a thriving concern with the surrounding farmers, who used the bar as a meeting place. After the closure of the railway in the sixties the name changed yet again to the Lord Nelson.

In the last 3 years major renovations and extensions have taken place with the additions of patios, porches and family rooms. Available within the next year, will be five letting rooms, all with en-suite facilites. These rooms have lain dormant for forty years, and during the renovations many original features were uncovered and have now been brought to life again.

A wide range of bar meals are available, including home made specialities, burgers, ploughmans, and sandwiches. The restaurant serves steaks, mixed grills, together with exotic duck in honey and lemon sauce, or chicken breasts filled with pate and maderia sauce. Perhaps try one of the home made specials such as beef and guiness pie or a traditional vegetarian favourite, macaroni cheese. All main meals are served with fresh vegetables and potatoes. Excellent value and well worth a visit.

USEFUL INFORMATION

OPEN: M-T:10.30-2.30pm,
   5.30-11.00pm. F-S: 10.30am-
   11pm. Sun: 12-3.00pm, 7-10.30pm
CHILDREN: Yes in the family room.
CREDIT CARDS: Access/Visa/
   Barclaycard.
LICENSED: Full licence.
GARDEN: Yes.

RESTAURANT: Homemade specials,
   steaks, chicken, duck, fish,
   sweets.
BAR FOOD: Homemade specials,
   Jacket potatoes, ploughmans,
   sandwiches, sweets.
VEGETARIAN: Yes, good selection
   in the bar and restuarant.
ACCESS FOR THE DISABLED:
   Level entrances.

THE LIME KILN INN

Inn

Long Sutton,
Nr. Langport, Somerset
Tel: (0458) 241242

Easily accessible from the M5 some 17 miles away, The Lime Kiln Inn is on the A372 just four miles off the A 303. It is ideally situated if you want to spend an afternoon loking at the Naval Air Museum at Yeovilton 4 miles away, or for a stroll around the delightful town of Somerton $2^1/_2$ miles distant.

The Lime Kiln Inn is so picturesque and welcoming that one needs no excuse for visiting it in its own right. It is 17th century and its old walls are covered in beautiful Ivy, rich in colour. Originally it was a Cider house and did not become a pub until the early part of this century. Now you can have the best of both worlds, a lovely old building, a pub brimful with character including an Inglenook fireplace, an A La Carte restaurant, and some excellent letting rooms with private facilities. Add to this the hospitable and friendly hosts, Clive and Lauren Williams, and you will find it hard to beat. Their staff have the same welcoming manner which has obviously rubbed off from the owners.

Lunchtime and evenings there is a Bar menu with a selection of good foods from soups to steaks. The A La Carte restaurant is open in the evenings when the chef offers a fine selection of home cooked food including some specials which are also available in the bar. Traditional Sunday Lunch is served in the Restaurant – a delectable meal, beautifully cooked.

USEFUL INFORMATION

OPEN: 11.30-2.30pm, 5.30-Midnight. Open all day in Summer
CHILDREN: In restaurant
CREDIT CARDS: Access/ Mastercard/Visa/Eurocard
LICENSED: Full licence
GARDEN: 2 garden areas for eating & drinking

RESTAURANT: A La Carte
BAR FOOD: From soup to steak,lasagne etc
VEGETARIAN: 3-4 dishes daily
ACCESS FOR THE DISABLED: Yes, no special facilities

North Cadbury,
Nr. Yeovil, Somerset
Tel: (0963) 40248

THE CATASH INN
Public House

Situated half a mile north of the A 303 between Sparkford and Wincanton, in the village of North Cadbury, is the 200 year old Catash Inn. A delightful port of call for all sorts of reasons. one of which will no doubt be curiosity about its name which originated because it was situated in The Hundred of Catash. These 'Hundreds' of which there is a group situated around Catash, were territorial divisions on which originally one hundred families were settled, possibly soldiers in a conquered country. It was all a very long time ago and probably originated by the Danes.

Today The Catash will welcome you cordially into its midst. It has everything to make a visitor happy: good beer, excellent traditional ales, and a menu ranging from bar snacks to grills. Clive and Sandra Robinson are mine hosts and not only are they a friendly pair but they have a fund of stories about the pub and the area. There is also some comfortable accommodation. It is one of those places to which you will want to return.

When you order your food from the well chosen menu, you can rest assured everything that is put in front of you will be home cooked and using as much fresh and local produce as possible. Any lover of wine will be delighted at the wide range from many different countries, and all at sensible prices. Sunday lunch is very popular here and it is advisable to book in advance.

USEFUL INFORMATION

OPEN: 11.30-2.30pm. 6.30-11pm. Sun: 12-3pm. 7-10.30pm
CHILDREN: Welcome
CREDIT CARDS: Access/Visa
LICENSED: Full. Large selection of wines
GARDEN: Yes. Steam railway. Play tree. Tables & chairs

RESTAURANT: A La Carte. Grills a speciality
BAR FOOD: Bar snacks and daily specials
VEGETARIAN: 10 dishes daily
ACCESS FOR THE DISABLED: Not at the moment

THE MANOR ARMS
Restaurant & Public House

North Perrott,
Nr. Crewkerne, Somerset
Tel: (0460) 72901

The Manor Arms is a Grade II Listed building, full of olde worlde charm and character. The only pub and restaurant in North Perrott, it overlooks the green in this lovely hamstone village, which has recently been made a preservation area. North Perrott, including the Manor Arms, was owned by the Hoskyns family and their descendants still live in the village. You will see the Hoskyns family crest is still in use on the pub signs. Indeed there are regular users of the pub who can still remember when one of the two bars was used only by the gentry and the other by the farm workers.

This 16th century building has been lovingly restored and refurbished by Rex and Jane Gilmore, the owners, retaining and enhancing many of the original features such as the inglenook fireplace. The Manor offers friendly service in comfortable surroundings with a choice of home made dishes, and is able to offer also bed and breakfast, en suite in the adjacent coach house. You will find it, approaching either from Yeovil or Crewkerne, opposite the village green on the main A3066 Bridport road. The menus in the Bar and Restaurant are unpretentious combining typical English fayre with more original dishes such as Chicken cooked with fresh oranges and tarragon or salmon wrapped in puff pastry with an asparagus and prawn sauce. The Bar menu has equally exciting dishes and both are very reasonably priced offering great value for money. On Sundays there is an excellent traditional three course lunch.

USEFUL INFORMATION

OPEN: Food: 12-2.00pm, 7-9.45pm. Pub: M-S: 11.30-2.30pm. 6.30-11.00pm, Sun:12-2.30pm, 7-10.30pm.
CHILDREN: Yes. Adventure playground
CREDIT CARDS: Visa/Access/ Euro/Mastercard
LICENSED: Full On Licence/Supper Lic.

GARDEN: Beer Garden. Adventure playground
RESTAURANT: Trad. & Original. Home-made
BAR FOOD: Good value for money menu
VEGETARIAN: 3/4 dishes daily
ACCESS FOR THE DISABLED: One step down

North Street, Shepton Beauchamp,
Nr. Ilminster, Somerset

Tel: (0460) 40314

DUKE OF YORK
Public House

In this charming village with its mellow honey-coloured houses, there is only one pub. Originally 16th century, the Duke of York has been a hostelry for three hundred years. It is full of atmosphere and has been made a happy place by the landlords, Roy and Jackie Spendlow. It is a free house, with hanging baskets galore, a nice beer garden, a skittle alley and good beer.

It is said that it is haunted by a ghost who walks the top landing. He is probably only too delighted to spirit such a nice establishment and listen to the fun and the enjoyment of good food. All the staff are local people and the bar is always home to a number of locals. English home cooking has become the hallmark of the Duke of York. You get delicious Oxtail Stews, Steak and Kidney Pies with pastry that melts in the mouth, thick home-made soups and crusty bread as an example.

There are many more dishes on the A La Carte menu but if you prefer to stick to the Bar Food Menu, the home-made beefburgers are particularly good. Two delicious pies are on offer as well, a Fisherman's Pie made from fish caught by the landlord or a succulent Cottage Pie, plus much more.

USEFUL INFORMATION

OPEN: 12-3.00pm, 6.30-11.00pm. Sun: 12-3.00pm, 7-10.30pm.
CHILDREN: Yes. Childrens Room
CREDIT CARDS: None taken
LICENSED: Full Licence
GARDEN: Yes. Shrubs & Lawn. Car Park

RESTAURANT: English Home Cooking
BAR FOOD: Wide range.
VEGETARIAN: Yes, Lasagne, Curries etc.
ACCESS FOR THE DISABLED: No

THE ROYAL OAK
Public House

Stoke St Gregory,
Taunton, Somerset
Tel: (0823) 490602

The Royal Oak is in the centre of the village just opposite St Gregory's Church. It is an interesting part of the Somerset Levels, well known for the growing of Withys which are used in the local craft of basket and furniture making, and also produces sticks of charcoal.

Dave and Cathy Bennatto, the landlords of this nice Free House, have given the pub an extensive refurbishment. There is a three level lounge bar with beams and balustrades which capture the olde worlde feeling. A separate games bar with a family room at the rear leads onto a patio area and garden. It is reputed to be haunted by a resident ghost but the Benattos have not seen it in the $2\frac{1}{2}$ years that they have been there.

Food is high on the list of priorities in this friendly establishment, providing everything from the humble sausage and chips to Trout garnished with almonds, and Chargrilled steaks. One of the specialities of the house is a Fish Crumble which is delicious. On Sundays traditional roasts with all the trimmings and tempting sweets are served from 12 noon until last food orders at 2pm. All meals are cooked freshly on Sunday mornings, and this has ensured that the Royal Oak's reputation is high. It is advisable to book a table in advance to avoid disappointment.

USEFUL INFORMATION

OPEN: Weekdays: 11-30-3.00pm,
6.30-11.00pm Sun: 12-3.00pm.
7-10.30pm
CHILDREN: Family room
CREDIT CARDS: None
LICENSED: Supper Licence applied
for
GARDEN: Patio area & Garden

RESTAURANT: Not applicable
BAR FOOD: Good value. Good food
VEGETARIAN: 2 dishes daily
ACCESS FOR THE DISABLED: Yes

HAYMAKER INN

Wadeford,
Nr. Chard, Somerset
Tel: (0460) 63349

Inn

Quite close to Chard and in the most peaceful scenic rural setting is the Haymaker Inn. It is renowned for its warmth and hospitality and is a regular port of call for locals and for people coming and going to the coast which is only 20 minutes away. There is much of interest surrounding it especially two old mills, Hornsbury and Perry Cider. The area has a good reputation for rambling, so for those who like a good walk before or after lunch it is ideal. Guests are welcome to stay here with three delightfully furnished letting rooms available.

The Haymaker has been a pub for more than 250 years, recently acquiring its present name in 1972, and has that nice solid, old English interior, complete with the traditional open fires, that creates character. The regular visitors have made Skittles a popular pastime and they boast a number of keen darts players who are always willing to give you a game. On warm summer days great fun can also be had playing petangue down at the bottom of garden, and for Children there is 'Herbie the tree'!

In the bar you can choose from a wide assortment of good, home cooked fare ranging from grills to salads or toasted sandwiches. Each day produces something different as a 'special'. The steak and kidney pie is particularly good. The restaurant offers delicious food in the French manner. Perhaps start with Deep fried Brie with a Gooseberry sauce or Escargots. Follow that with a succulent duck and you have a feast. Sunday lunch is traditional both in the bar and restaurant. It is always advisable to book a table in the restaurant on any day.

USEFUL INFORMATION

OPEN: Win: 6-11.00pm, Sum: 11-2.30pm, 5-11.00pm
CHILDREN: Very welcome
CREDIT CARDS: Access/Visa/ Mastercard
LICENSED: Full licence. Real Ale
GARDEN: Yes. 'Herbie' the tree. Climbing frame. Barbeque, Skittle Alley.

RESTAURANT: Yes. French/English cuisine
BAR FOOD: Hot Platters. Jacket potatoes. Sandwiches. Salads, Burgers etc
VEGETARIAN: Yes. At least 4 dishes daily
ACCESS FOR THE DISABLED: No, none at all

THE FOUR ACRES HOTEL
Hotel with Restaurant

West Coker,
Yeovil, Somerset.
Tel: (0935) 862555/6

Full of character and set in beautifully landscaped grounds, the elegant Four Acres country house hotel is an extremely popular venue. Unlike all too many modern hotels which can be clinical, impersonal and uninviting, the mainly 18th century Four Acres has a warm, homely and welcoming atmosphere. It offers a perfect blend of old world charm and courtesy, tranquil surroundings, modern amenities, excellent cuisine and first class service.

The hotel's restaurant is called the Bingham Room and can seat ninety for dinner. The head chef makes sure that the use of oil and dairy products in the preparation and cooking of meat, poultry, fish and vegetables is kept to a minimum but in taking care of the health of his valued clientele, he does not in any way detract from the subtle tastes and flavours in every dish that he creates.

Bar snacks and meals, including chef's dish of the day, are readily available. In the Bingham Room, you can feast on a range of starters including La salade Marie-Lou, a delicious salad with spinach, poached egg and three roses of smoked Salmon followed by John Dory fillets with a white wine sauce or Le Pot-au-feu de Canard aux Petits Legumes, a mouth watering Duck stew garnished with Vegetables. The dessert trolley will tempt you too. On Sundays there is a first class traditional lunch.

USEFUL INFORMATION

OPEN: All year. Res't/Bar: 12-2.00pm
CHILDREN: Welcome
CREDIT CARDS: Amex/Diners/
Visa/Mastercard
LICENSED: Fully Licenced
GARDEN: Yes. Food/drink can be
served outside in the summer.

RESTAURANT: English/French
cuisine
BAR FOOD: Available during bar
opening hours
VEGETARIAN: Yes 3-4 dishes
ACCESS FOR THE DISABLED: Yes.
6 ground floor level rooms

142 Preston Road,
Yeovil, Somerset
Tel: (0935) 76566

THE PLUCKNETT HOTEL
Pub, Restaurant, Inn

Andy Puttock and Robert Bartrupp are two entertaining and talented men who make perfect hosts for the Victorian Plucknett Hotel. The former is an ex county champion tennis player and Robert was a horticultural consultant who helped his previous company win gold medals at the Chelsea Flower Show. This may not seem a natural progression towards becoming successful hoteliers and innkeepers but their innovative, imaginative personalities have certainly made The Plucknett a place to visit.

Not everyone loves them; the 350 years old cellar is haunted by a monk who does not like the idea of the pub being built on the site of his old monastery. He is quite harmless though and merely adds to the general interest of the establishment. When you visit this nice pub you will find the food is the best of English and Continental fare and the Real Ale is up to the standard required by any enthusiast. It is an ideal spot for a small wedding reception, company meetings or private parties; with some well appointed guest rooms available for those wishing to stay and included in the reasonable cost is full english breakfast.

The assortment of starters are popular ones and well prepared such as the prawn, celery and apple cocktail or the chef's own pate. To follow, the a la carte menu offers for example: a variety of succulent steaks which can just be grilled or served with a sauce; fresh salmon in an asparagus sauce, and roast duckling, plus much more. The bar menu has a home made dish of the day with fresh vegetables, wonderful home made soups and an endless array of other dishes. On Sunday there is always roast beef and either pork or lamb plus delicious home made sweets. A limited a la carte and vegetarian menus are also available.

USEFUL INFORMATION

OPEN: 11-3.00pm, 6-11.00pm, Sun:
   12-3.00pm, 7-10.30pm
CHILDREN: Yes in Back bar &
   Restaurant
CREDIT CARDS: All major cards
LICENSED: Full Licence
GARDEN: Well appointed &
   Childrens area.

RESTAURANT: A La Carte
BAR FOOD: Special,varied bar menu
VEGETARIAN: Yes. 5 dishes
ACCESS FOR THE DISABLED:
   Catered for Restaurant & Bar

THE RAILWAY HOTEL
Hotel/Inn

63 Hendford Hill,
Yeovil, Somerset
Tel: (0935) 75835

For a substantial, wholesome meal at very low prices, The Railway Hotel is hard to beat. It is also situated at the foot of Hendford Hill which borders on a local beauty spot 'Ninesprings'. Alan and Margaret Crowe, who are the landlords, know that it was built about 1766 but the earliest recorded date of the pub is 1851. They would be delighted to hear from anyone who has any information about its earlier history. The building has had additions over the years and suffered bombing in World War II when it was a favourite haunt for American servicemen. Indeed, it was these men who rebuilt the skittle alley enjoyed by so many today.

A new kitchen has recently been added in which the tempting home-made casseroles, hot pots, roasts and pies are cooked. They are all served, at lunch time, with a selection of potatoes and fresh vegetables. Nothing costs more than £3 – incredible value.

In the evenings you can enjoy succulent steaks up to 20oz in weight served with vegetables and a side salad from £5. On Sundays a traditional lunch is available with a choice of roast meats, crisp roast potatoes and fresh vegetables, followed by a sweet and coffee. This is essentially a nice family run pub where Alan and Margaret are helped by their daughters Jackie and Rachel.

USEFUL INFORMATION

OPEN: Daily:11-11.00pm
Sun:12-3.00pm, 7-10.30pm
CHILDREN: Limited facility
CREDIT CARDS: None taken
LICENSED: Real Ales, Keg Beers.
Small choice of wines
GARDEN: Patio with tables & chairs.

RESTAURANT: Not applicable
BAR FOOD: Good home cooked
food.
VEGETARIAN: On request
ACCESS FOR THE DISABLED:
with help

THE RED HOUSE INN
Inn

Dorchester Road,
Yeovil, Somerset

Tel: (0935) 77744

This is one of the most attractive pubs in the area. It is very old, full of charm and friendliness and over the years has been very skillfully modernised. Within its decorative walls is a comfortable sixty seater restaurant in which you can eat delicious and well presented food. If you are there in the evening for dinner you may well find the additional bonus of being entertained with live music. There is something especially nice about the atmosphere in The Red House which accounts for its popularity locally and also brings people back there time and again once they have discovered it. It is quite easily found on the main road to Dorchester.

Every day in the bar there is a big blackboard which proclaims the specials of the day. They are always home cooked, plentiful and very good value for money. In addition there are basket meals, platters, pate, freshly cut sandwiches and a whole host of tempting items. It would be very difficult not to find something that would tempt your taste buds.

The restaurant has a slightly more sophisticated menu and the waitress service is excellent. There is a wide range of starters including crispy whitebait. The fish dishes are tempting, chicken is served in a variety of ways and the steaks, cooked perfectly, come from a local butcher. Probably one of the best value meals of all is the Carvery where the roast meats on offer are fresh every day and served with a selection of seasonal fresh vegetables and a choice of potatoes. The desserts will please anyone with a sweet tooth.

USEFUL INFORMATION

OPEN: 11-11.00pm. Sun: 12-3.00pm. 7-10.30pm
CHILDREN: Yes, very welcome
CREDIT CARDS: Visa/Access/ Diners/Eurocard
LICENSED: Full Licence
GARDEN: Yes. Play area. Tables & chairs

RESTAURANT: Carvery. Fish. Grills, steaks
BAR FOOD: English food. Specials. Basket meals
VEGETARIAN: 5-6 dishes daily
ACCESS FOR THE DISABLED: Level entrance at back

Vicar's Close, Wells, The most complete Mediaeval street in Europe.

INCLUDES:

"Some have meat and cannot eat,
Some cannot eat that want it;
But we have meat and we can eat,
Sae let the Lord be thankit."
Robert Burns

Glastonbury *beckons but having just left North Cadbury, I cannot miss out* **Bruton** *which has such charm. Not the least of its attractions is a picturesque packhorse bridge which crosses the River Brue. It is directly opposite the west end of* the churchyard leading to the impressive two-towered church. The north tower is not particularly notable but the later 15th-century west tower soars, with pinnacled buttresses and window shafts. Both Charles I and Charles II, whose arms are over the north door, stayed in Bruton and worshipped in this church. It is a bustling place made to appear even busier than it is because of its narrow streets.

It is because of the legends that Glastonbury is such a place of pilgrimage. The town may well disappoint you but not the famous TOR which stands out for miles as you travel about Somerset. It is a conical hill with the remains of St Michaels church on the top, the effort of climbing to which is rewarded by wonderful views. CHALICE WELL lies at the foot of the Tor. Arthurian legend links it with healing and the quest for the Holy Grail. You can go there throughout the year but in winter only in the afternoons. Tradition tells us that Arthur and Guinevere were buried in Glastonbury and that Joseph of Arimathea came here to bring good news from Galilee. He thrust his staff into the ground in what is now the churchyard of the church of St John the Baptist, where it immediately burst into bloom – the Glastonbury Thorn.

The church is wonderful, its 134 ft 15th-century tower is the second tallest in the county. It is a church full of light, created by the tall nave arcades and clerestory, with shafts on angel corbels supporting the timber roof. The 15th-century stained glass in the chancel is exquisite. You can go into the church anyday between 8am-8pm except in winter when the church shuts at 6pm. You are bound to be hungry and thirsty after exploring so why not take yourself into THE RIFLEMANS ARMS.

Within the town there are some old houses which are worth looking at, the abbey ruins are a must. I like THE ABBEY BARN which is now the home of THE SOMERSET RURAL LIFE MUSEUM. It is a place of exploration with exhibits including hand tools and horse age machinery, rural crafts, cider making equipment and the art of peat digging.

Close to Glastonbury is **Street**, often ignored because it lives in the shadow of its renowned neighbour. Two families developed this quite ancient town: the Clarkes and the Morlands. Clarkes shoes have become world famous and it has a fascinating museum which displays shoes from

Roman times to the present day, also, a remarkable collection of snuff boxes, advertising posters, fashion plates, buckles and shoe making machinery of the 19th century. It is certainly different. The Morlands dealt in sheep skins and still do. In 1870 Morlands established a working tannery producing first quality skins and by 1906 with the revolutionary growth of the motor car, Morlands were manufacturing coats, rugs and footwarmers for the discerning motorist. As technology advanced so did the need for more practical ways of keeping warm. In 1919, Morlands started to make boots and slippers. Thirty years on, the company were supplying boots and jackets to the Air Force and, indeed, to the famous Sir Edmund Hilary, who made the first perilous ascent of Mount Everest. You can look for yourselves in Morland's factory shop to see what they do today. There is ample parking and it is open from Monday – Saturday from 9.30am-5pm.

The Ruins of Glastonbury Abbey

The cathedral city of **Wells** is exceptionally rich in its heritage of historic buildings, crowned by the awe inspiring Cathedral which must rank high in the examples of Gothic architecture in England. To wander through the town is to revel in its beauty. It has Vicar's Close, the most complete medieval street in Europe and the superb moated Bishop's Palace, still the residence of the Bishop of Bath and Wells, complete with swans who have inherited the trick of ringing a bell for food from their Victorian ancestors. The Palace Garden contains the wells from which the city gets its name. St Cuthbert, the largest parish church in Somerset *is also worth seeing. It is open during daylight hours every day. For a hospitable welcome before enjoying a good meal THE FOUNTAIN INN awaits you.*

*Two miles away from Wells on the A371 is WOOKEY HOLE CAVES which owe their existence to the River Axe. The underground river carved out the spectacular caverns and for 1000 years provided water power to riverside mills. The beauty of these extraordinary caves are dramatically revealed by brilliant lighting effects. A knowledgeable guide will take you on your half mile cave tour, illustrating the 50,000 years of history and legend from the earliest cave dwellers to the Celts and Romans. After you have explored the caves you can follow the unspoilt river valley to enjoy the attractions in THE VICTORIAN PAPER MILL. There is plenty of free parking, picnic areas and Wookey Hole Caves are open every day of the year except the week before Christmas. The times are 9.30am-5.30pm in summer and 10.30am-4.30pm in winter. THE WESTBURY INN at **Westbury-sub-Mendip** would be a welcoming place to visit after Wookey Hole.*

All aboard for the East Somerset Railway

*I have talked about three of the five Mendip towns so before going towards the coast I want to take you a little further east in this part of the county. **Shepton Mallet** first, which is the geographical and administrative centre of the district, and, of course, famous for its annual Agricultural show site. It is an interesting town with a fine market place and a 15th-century shambles at its heart. There are two places that will* *always bring me back to Shepton Mallet. The first is the church of St Peter and Paul with its amazing and unforgettable wagon roof of the 15th century with 350 carved panels and over 300 bosses, each one different and creating an overall floral effect. It is open daily from 8.45am until dusk. The second is THE CANNARD'S WELL INN at Cannard's Grave, a place deep rooted in history.*

On the road from Shepton Mallet to Frome you will pass the home of the little EAST SOMERSET RAILWAY on your right and CRANMORE TOWER on your left. The railway is known as The Strawberry Line and is one of only two 100% steam railways in the country. You will need to see the timetable for actual steam days but the trains are open for viewing from April to October daily from 10am-5.30pm To get more information ring (074 988) 417.

Frome *has several delightful places within easy distance.* **Mells** *is just 2 miles to the west. What a delightful village it is and is connected, albeit on flimsy grounds, with the nursery rhyme Little Jack Horner. Why, you may ask. The answer is simple: the Elizabethan manor house once belonged to the Horner family. The stone cottages are of grey and yellow stone, wreathed by trees and lawns. The church of St Andrew has a splendid 15th-century tower with triple windows. Every three hours one of four tunes is chimed. The church is open daily during daylight hours.*

Holcombe *is another lovely village with a wonderful pub, THE RING OF ROSES, to which I always return having spent just a little while thinking about the past when Captain Scott of Antartic fame, came to bury his father in the churchyard of the old church. His brother, sister and mother are also buried here. His mother must have had great courage. She died in Hampton Court Palace at the age of 84 but she did not want to be buried there. It was her wish to be brought to Holcombe, and be carried across the fields to be laid to rest in this peaceful place so far from her son who died in Antartica.*

Six miles to the north of the town is **Rode** *where THE TROPICAL BIRD GARDENS are laid out in 17 acres of beautiful grounds, terraced and planted many years ago with ornamental trees and shrubs now in full maturity which give shade and shelter. There are flower gardens, a Clematis collection, a wood inhabited with exquisitely coloured ornamental pheasants who wander round at liberty. There is a chain of lakes fed by a stream and water-fall where you will see all kinds of water birds swimming and diving, including Flamingoes and Penguins; Macaws fly free among the trees.*

The Aviaries, which are all outdoors, are designed to blend with the surroundings. They are naturally planted and so extensive that visitors can enjoy watching the birds in full flight and admire their brilliant colours as they flash in the sunshine. The collection which is constantly being added to, now numbers over 1,000 rare birds in approximately 230 different species. The gardens are open every day except Christmas Day. the times in summer are 10am-6.30pm and in winter from 10am until dusk.

I had one of the best steaks I have ever eaten at THE SPORTSMAN at Rode.

The Lions of Longleat

Frome is the largest of the five towns with a population of over 20,000. It has a number of picturesque streets such as Cheap Street and impressive buildings dating from the times when it was an important centre of the silk and woollen industries. It is in close proximity to LONGLEAT which must offer one of the best days out, whatever your age. It is a magnificent 16th-century house set in rolling parkland. It has priceless family heirlooms spanning four centuries. A safari park with lions, white tigers, monkeys, rhinos, wolves, zebras, giraffes. camels, buffalo and elephants. Fascinating exhibittons including the Doctor Who exhibition. There are rides, amusements and the world's largest maze. Adventure Castle is a 2 acre playpark which is a child's paradise. Spend a day here and you will be in good company. Queen Elizabeth I visited Sir John Thynne, the builder of the house in 1574, and in 1980

Queen Elizabeth II honoured the present Marquess of Bath, a direct descendant of Sir John's, by joining him in the celebration of the four hundredth anniversary of the completion of his home. Longleat is an architectural masterpiece in its own right. It is also home to one of the finest private book collections in the world. Longleat is open every day except Christmas Day from 10am-6pm Easter-September and 10am-4pm during the rest of the year.

If you wander the lanes to the west you will come to the sleepy hollow that envelops the village of **Litton**. *It is an old place with streets that are steep and winding. On the walls of the old church are four hideous gargoyles and two angels interspersed with about 30 stone heads amongst which are laughing men, some with beards and women wearing wimples. Inside there are ancient benches, a Jacobean pulpit and a 15th-century font. Appropriately the excellent village pub is called YE OLDE KINGS ARMS.*

Axbridge *church has some good brasses and glass. Also in Axbridge is the National Trust Property KING JOHN'S HUNTING LODGE. This medieval town house has retained its original half-timbered construction and it is a clear indication of Axbridge's position as a Royal Borough from the 9th to the 19th century. As well as being a fascinating building in its own right, the Lodge also houses AXBRIDGE MUSEUM. This informative exhibition provides a keen insight to local Prehistoric Roman and Medieval archaeology together with a number of changing displays. Open daily from 2-5pm April to September.*

Cheddar *has to be the next stop. One tends to forget how pretty the village is. It is the home of Cheddar Cheese of course but most people come here to see the Gorge. It is an attraction of outstanding natural beauty. Cheddar Showcaves offer a fascinating day out. The beautiful rock formation in the caves have taken over half a million years to form and are carefully lit to show off their jewel-like beauty. The Gorge is an important conservation area because of its rare flowers and spectacular sheer limestone cliffs. Gough's Cave, the largest, was first dug open in 1892 by a colourful old sea-captain, Richard Gough. Today, well lit pathways will take you deep into the enormous, cathedral like caverns to reveal wonderful stalagmites and stalactites of incredible beauty. Cox's Cave is small, but prettier with its 'Mirror' pools of water reflecting the burnished gold of rock formations. It was the first cave to be discovered and opened. Jacob's Ladder is an energetic climb up 274 steps to the top of the cliffs. Illustration points on the way up describe how the world has evolved, and give you a chance to catch your breath! On top of the cliffs the views are fantastic. From Prospect Tower you can*

81

look across the Somerset Levels, and a short walk takes you to Pulpit Rock for dramatic views down into the Gorge itself.

After seeing the Gorge the Showcaves and THE RURAL CHEDDAR GORGE VILLAGE where the 1920's style village allows you to step back to a more leisurely age when there was time to watch the bread bake, the cheese mature and enjoy the fruits of one's own labours, you will be ready for a drink in THE GALLERIES INN in Cheddar itself.

Wedmore *found fame when coins buried in the 11th century in the churchyard by a man who was looking for the safest place, were discovered early this century and removed to the British Museum. I wonder why he never came back for them? Another treasure here is THE BOROUGH VENTURE where the landlord and the locals will give you much more history of this ancient village.*

The Cliffs,
The Gorge, Cheddar, Somerset
Tel: (0934) 742584

THE GALLERIES INN
Restaurant, Inn

Cheddar Gorge is one of the most exciting places in the South West. A lot of time and energy is expended by visitors who are thrilled by the Showcaves, The Cheddar Cheese Village and the many attractions; but the wise ones know that to find refreshment and relaxation and a means of recharging ones batteries, there is no better place to visit than The Galleries Inn. The attractive garden and extensive patio areas are right on the main Gorge road. It is immediately next to the 'Park and Ride' Pick up point.

It has only been an Inn for some 20 years but most of the building has stood for well over 150 years. It has grown a character and atmosphere all its own with a little help from Bob and Jo Poole and John Spence, who are the proprietors. They are friendly, welcoming people who run The Galleries efficiently but as informally as possible. Their staff follow their lead. The chef is excellent, he has over 20 years experience in catering at various hotels and restaurants in Somerset; you will discover his ability when you taste the food. You can eat either in the bar or in the restaurant. The food is all home-made. Bar snacks are delicious and imaginative with dishes such as seafood pies or ratatouille. The Ploughmans are particularly good and are served with the locally made cheese, of course. In the restaurant, try the Shark steak in Blue Curacao or Somerset Rabbit from the wide range of dishes available. During the winter months there is always a traditional roast lunch on Sundays.

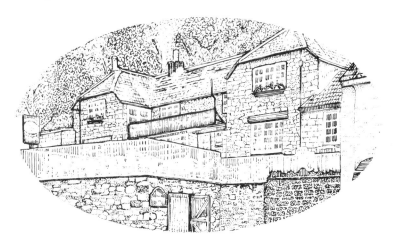

USEFUL INFORMATION

OPEN: 11-3.30pm 6-11.00pm (Food all day)
CHILDREN: Limited facilities.
CREDIT CARDS: None taken
LICENSED: Full Licence. Varied selection of Real Ales
GARDEN: 2 Beer patios + terrace, 75 seats

RESTAURANT: Variety & quality at pub prices
BAR FOOD: All home cooked, served at table. Children's menu available.
VEGETARIAN: Extensive 10 + options
ACCESS FOR THE DISABLED: None

THE RIFLEMANS ARMS
Public House

4, Chilkwell Street,
Glastonbury, Somerset
Tel: (0458) 31023

It is rare in this day to find a true Ale House but that is exactly what The Riflemans Arms is in the true sense. Seek it out and you will discover this delightful place is in the old world tradition; inside the nice character bar has low beamed ceilings and a large fireplace which makes it warm and cheerful in the cold winter months. John Simpson has been the landlord here for five years and he has nurtured the Ale House image, fighting against any suggestion of modernising it and so losing its charm. Instead the public rooms have been extended in keeping with the main bar area and so preserving a building which is thought to date back several centuries. If you take a close look at the stone mullion windows you will discover they were taken from the Abbey buildings at the time of the dissolution of the monasteries.

A good pub to visit at anytime it is particularly attractive on Tuesdays when most people frequent the town centre pubs because it is market day. It is only three miles down the road beside the A361 from Shepton Mallett and is within easy distance of both The Abbey and The Tor. Its tranquil air welcomes you after the hustle and bustle of market day and you can be assured of a first class pint and simple but good meal served daily between 12-2pm. Particularly good is the home-made soup of the day with crispy French bread and butter. If you are a vegetarian there is a splendid Vegeburger in a bun with garnish. Hot roast beef in French bread is another favourite as are the Bacon and Mushroom Baps. Good wholesome food at reasonable prices.

USEFUL INFORMATION

OPEN: 11-2.30pm 5-11.00pm
CHILDREN: Childrens Room
CREDIT CARDS: None
LICENSED: Full Licence
GARDEN: Patio area seats 100

RESTAURANT: Wholesome. Home cooked food
BAR FOOD: Wide range
VEGETARIAN: Yes. Approx 6 dishes
ACCESS FOR THE DISABLED: Yes

RING O' ROSES

Public House

Stratton Road,
Holcombe, Nr Bath, Avon

Tel: (0761) 232478

Even if it were not for this nice pub, Holcombe would be interesting. There have been two villages here, the first was destroyed by the plague, and the second was subsequently built a little way from it, this unfortunately left the original church in total isolation in a field, to be used only occasionally in summer. It was here that Scott of the Antartic worshipped and his family lie buried in the churchyard. Halfway between the two villages is where you will find the Ring O' Roses.

This Grade II listed building was once a farmhouse and has been standing for 200 years. It is full of character with not only a nice bar and an attractive restaurant but 4 letting bedrooms. Here you can stay either to enjoy the wonderful country-side or explore the incomparable beauty of Bath which is nearby. The famous Downside Abbey is closeby too and makes an excellent place to visit after enjoying the hospitality and food of Brian and Jenny Whittlesey and their son who is the chef. It is he who cooks the tempting meals on the well balanced menu. His Pork Pepperoni, Roast Duckling and Steak au Poivre are known for miles around. There is a full range of bar meals and vegetarians are not forgotten. Sunday lunch is a feast of either Roast Beef or Turkey alternating with Chicken and Lamb.

USEFUL INFORMATION

OPEN: Mon-Sat: 10.30-3.00pm, 6-11.00pm. Sun: 12-3.00pm, 7-10.30pm.
CHILDREN: Welcome
CREDIT CARDS: None taken
LICENSED: Full Licence
GARDEN: Yes. Pets corner planned

RESTAURANT: Home-made dishes + steaks
BAR FOOD: Bar menu + daily specials
VEGETARIAN: Yes
ACCESS FOR THE DISABLED: No

YE OLDE KINGS ARMS
Public House

Litton,
Nr. Bath, Somerset
Tel: (0761) 21301

On the B 3114, seven miles north of Shepton Mallet is Ye Olde Kings Arms, an Inn not to be missed. Built in the 15th century it has a pantiled roof, brilliant white facade and black painted woodwork. Inside, the impression of its great age hits you. The stone floors shine with the patina of years, the large open fireplaces light up the low-beamed ceilinged rooms and spell out a welcome. The defeated Charles II, disguised as a servant, Will Jackson, stayed here in 1651 after the Battle of Worcester, on his way to loyal friends endeavouring to engineer his flight from the country. The welcome rest it assured him can still be found today.

Take note of the enormous oak settle near the door. It must have been constructed in the house and nearby is a massive oak table with a highly polished surface marked out for what could have been the forerunner of Shove-halfpenny. In this wonderful atmosphere you are invited to lunch, wine and dine or merely to enjoy a snack and a coffee. The pub is renowned for its selection of fine ales, including several traditional beers, good wines, malt whiskies and its excellent food.

There is always a good selection of hot and cold dishes, some wonderful seafood dishes and home made pies. For vegetarians the dishes are definitely different. Sandwiches are fresh and filling. If you are in a hurry you are asked to say so when you place your order. On Sundays there is a first class carvery as well as the usual menu. Ideal venue for weddings, business meetings, auctions, seminars etc and you can stay here in well appointed rooms.

USEFUL INFORMATION

OPEN: Weekdays: 11-3.00pm.
6-11.00pm. Sun: 12-3.00pm.
7-11.00pm
CHILDREN: Yes, in 2 rooms
CREDIT CARDS: Access/Visa
LICENSED: Full Licence
GARDEN: Yes, 3 acres spacious
lawns & flowers.

RESTAURANT: Extensive menu.
Steaks & Seafood.
BAR FOOD: Good selection hot and
cold food
VEGETARIAN: Several dishes daily
ACCESS FOR THE DISABLED: Yes

24, Bradford Road,
Rode, Nr. Bath, Avon
Tel: (0373) 830249/830468

THE SPORTSMAN STEAKHOUSE
Steakhouse

In charming countryside just 4 miles from Bradford on Avon is The Sportsman Steakhouse at Rode. The building is three hundred years old and once was an old working barn. Perhaps not the most exciting place to look at outside, old working barns rarely are, but once through the doors you will find it a charming eatery with a pleasant, intimate atmosphere.

The menu naturally includes steaks which are prime cuts ready to be grilled to your liking. An enormous T Bone steak will cost you just £9.50 which is excellent value. There is a sizeable mixed grill, Lamb Chops, Liver, Bacon and Onions as well as Gammon Steak or half a chicken with sauce. You might prefer to try the home-made specialities like Tipsy Pigeon or Pheasant Casserole or perhaps some fish. Grilled Trout, Lemon Sole, Scampi in breadcrumbs or a delicious smoked mackerel with salad. There are Appetisers as well and a tempting selection of sweets.

On Sundays in addition to the normal menu you can enjoy a beautifully cooked and presented traditional lunch possibly accompanied by one of the very fairly priced wines from the list. There is a particularly good Australian Hunter Valley cabernet sauvignon which goes down very well with Roast Beef. A thoroughly enjoyable visit and good value for money.

USEFUL INFORMATION

OPEN: Daily 12-2.00pm,
    6.30-11.00pm Sun. Eve:
    7-11.00pm
CHILDREN: Very welcome
CREDIT CARDS: Access/Visa
LICENSED: Restaurant licence
GARDEN: Roof Garden, extension to
    bar

RESTAURANT: Good home cooking
BAR FOOD: Not applicable
VEGETARIAN: Yes
ACCESS FOR THE DISABLED: Yes

CANNARDS WELL INN

Inn

Cannards Grave,
Shepton Mallet, Somerset
Tel: (0749) 346247/344513

Just over a year ago Clive and Sharon King took over the 16th-century Cannard's Well Inn which stands on the junction of the A37 and A361 in the Mendips, just outside the market town of Shepton Mallett. It is an inn steeped in local history, at one end of the bar is a toft well, which is said to be of Roman origin. Certainly a Roman fortress was found about 500 yards from the pub. At the other end of the bar is the grave of Tom Giles, the last person in Shepton to be hung for sheep stealing. He has been seen walking the corridors and bedrooms of the pub ever since!

In the last twelve months the Cannard's Well has become steadily more and more popular. It is not just the excellence of the food, it is the happy, friendly atmosphere that prevails. Clive has a fund of good stories and his laughter once heard will never be forgotten. Sharon helps their excellent chef, Ivor Cross, in the kitchen; her speciality is curry. Ivor is well known for his presentation of good home-cooked food. In addition to the food and drink, there are 15 pleasant rooms for bed and breakfast – the latter is cooked by Clive and is an English breakfast of gargantuan proportion. Diners can eat in the Cottage Restaurant or in the bar. The bar menu, full of home-cooked dishes, is changed regularly and blackboard specials are changed daily. A separate a la carte menu operates in the Cottage Restaurant offering succulent and interesting dishes. On Sundays, Ivor's roast lunch is served from noon and is so popular that it is essential to book early.

USEFUL INFORMATION

OPEN: Mon-Sat: 11-2.30pm.
6-11.00pm Sun: 12-3.00pm.
7-10.30pm
CHILDREN: Under strict control of parents
CREDIT CARDS: Visa/Access/
Mastercard/Eurocard
LICENSED: Full Licence
GARDEN: Patio

RESTAURANT: Good home cooked food, full a la carte menu
BAR FOOD: Comprehensive bar menu. Daily chef's specials
VEGETARIAN: 4 dishes
ACCESS FOR THE DISABLED: No

THE BOROUGH VENTURE
Restauramt & Fashion Shop

Wedmore,
Somerset
Tel: (0934) 712779

Wedmore is one of the most charming villages in the whole of Somerset and in choosing The Borough Venture as a venue for a meal you are entering into a new experience. It is essentially a dress shop set in a pretty Gothic revivial style cottage built about 1800 which still has its original doors and windows. It is renowned throughout the South of England for its superb range of garments from some of Europe's leading design houses.

Within this attractive and intimate cottage atmosphere there is a delightful coffee shop which gives you an excellent reason for lingering. If the day is warm then you may be tempted to take your morning coffee, luncheon or afternoon tea in the seclusion of the pretty gardens.

The menu is refreshingly different. It takes into account the needs of slimmers and vegetarians whilst satisfying the very hungry. Everything is fresh and home-cooked. The Coffee shop is licensed so that you can enjoy a glass of wine, sherry or perhaps a lager or beer with your meal. On festive days such as Bastille Day and American Independence day you will find a special menu to mark the occasion and sometimes, whilst you are enjoying the excellent food, the appropriate national styles are modelled for your pleasure. There is a nice atmosphere about the whole building and no sense of pressure to do anything other than have a cup of coffee or a meal if that is what you wish. Many people are happy to spend the whole day here. The menu is refreshingly simple with 'Specials' available every day.

USEFUL INFORMATION

OPEN: 9.30-4.45pm
Monday-Saturday
CHILDREN: Yes. Children's Den
CREDIT CARDS: Access/
Barclaycard
LICENSED: Wines & Beers
GARDEN: Yes

RESTAURANT: Home cooked,
English & International
BAR FOOD: Not applicable
VEGETARIAN: Yes
ACCESS FOR THE DISABLED: Yes

THE FOUNTAIN INN & BOXERS RESTAURANT

Public House & Restaurant

1, St Thomas Street,
Wells, Somerset
Tel: (0749) 72317

Adrian and Sarah Lawrence have been the proprietors of this very nice establishment for 10 years, and have built up an enviable reputation for food and wine using only the very best of local produce. If you happen to love cheese you will be in your element; they have an award for their selection of West Country cheeses. The Fountain is situated on the junction of the B 3139 to Bath and A371 to Shepton Mallet, just 50 yards from Wells Cathedral, surrounded by many beautiful buildings, and after lunch what better pursuit than to wander around the moat to the Bishop's Palace.

The inn was built during the 16th century to house builders working on the cathedral. The bar is panelled and full of atmosphere with many pictures of local interest. Above the bar is Boxers Restaurant, furnished attractively, with pine tables and Laura Ashley decor. The pub is also surrounded by many excellent guest houses and bed and breakfast establishments.

Food, Glorious Food! A full menu of Bar Food is served every day of the week, lunchtime and evenings. Boxers Restaurant is open every evening and for Sunday lunch: a very popular meal for which it is advisable to arrive early. You will find delicious home-cooked food prepared from the finest ingredients catering for all tastes and budgets. There are Vegetarian dishes and a children's menu. The blackboard of chef's specials usually has 6 starters, 6 main courses and various fish dishes. The Fountain is one of the nicest and friendliest places in this beautiful Cathedral City.

USEFUL INFORMATION

OPEN: Weekdays: 10.30-2.30pm 6-11.00pm. Sun: 12-3.00pm, 7-10.30pm
CHILDREN: Welcome. Own menu.
CREDIT CARDS: Visa/Access/ Amex
LICENSED: Full Licence
GARDEN: No

RESTAURANT: Anglo-French using local produce
BAR FOOD: Wide range as restaurant
VEGETARIAN: Approx 7 dishes daily.
ACCESS FOR THE DISABLED: Yes, toilets on 1st floor

Westbury-sub-Mendip,
Wells, Somerset

Tel: (0749) 870223

THE WESTBURY INN
Village Pub

Westbury-sub-Mendip is an ideal stopping off point for visiting several super places. It is positioned almost centrally between the Wookey Hole Caves and Cheddar Gorge. It is close to England's smallest Cathedral City, Wells, and equally close to Glastonbury with its wonderful Abbey and historic Tor. The Northern part of Sedgemoor, famous for its battles, is right on the doorstep. With all this to see, The Westbury Inn is an ideal venue in which to have an excellent lunch or dinner.

This genuine village pub, which has been licensed for almost two hundred years, still retains the original slabbed floor in the dining area. You have to watch out for your heads because the doors are low and there are beams everywhere. It creates a wonderful atmosphere enhanced by Peter and Maureen Bond, who are experienced innkeepers in the very best tradition. They are the most helpful of couples who not only make you very welcome in their own establishment but will also go out of their way to find you suitable, comfortable accommodation in some of the best guest houses for miles. Food is ordered at the bar but table service is operated. The A la carte menu provides a range of 60 dishes to choose from and every meal is cooked to order. The daily specials are displayed on a blackboard. Twenty years of catering has made Maureen Bond justifiably proud in particular of her omelettes and preparation of seafood. The Scotch beef steaks are especially good as well. This is a happy, friendly pub and one to savour.

USEFUL INFORMATION

OPEN: Mon-Sat:11am-11.00pm.
  Sun:12-2.30pm, 7-10.30pm Last
  Food Orders: 2pm & 9pm
CHILDREN: Welcome in dining area
CREDIT CARDS: Not accepted
LICENSED: Full Licence
GARDEN: Patio at front. Rear
  Garden with tables

RESTAURANT: Not applicable
BAR FOOD: A choice of 60 A la carte
  dishes
VEGETARIAN: Four dishes daily
ACCESS FOR THE DISABLED: Not
  for wheelchairs

The famous Christmas Steps, Bristol

INCLUDES:

*"I went on a diet, swore off drinking and heavy eating,
and in fourteen days I lost two weeks."*

Joe. E. Lewis

Bristol's *geographical position has made it a place of import-*
ance over centuries. Each of which has added charm to this
major city of the west, nor has it ever tried to emulate its larger
cousins. In fact, Bristolians would be insulted to be thought
of in the same league as London, Birmingham or Manchester. The
15th century saw it as a time of sea-faring drama, the 17th and 18th
were blighted by the slave trade, civil wars and the arrogance of
the merchants. The turn of the 18th and 19th century was a time of
growth, new buildings appeared alongside the old. Clifton was grow-
ing, Kingsdown was a pleasant residential area. Whilst you are in
Kingsdown *incidentally, why not pop into THE BELL INN. All the*
while, Bristol's prosperity was still largely dependant on what happened
around the waterfront. Whilst much of this has changed there is no better
place to start an exploration of this historic and fascinating city than in
its **dockland area**.

First of all, let me tell you of a few places where you can refresh
yourselves at the end of a tour of discovery. THE RIVERSIDE CAFE is
right down on the docks, MULLIGANS FISH RESTAURANT lies
in the centre close by THE OLD CASTLE GREEN, THE CHINA
PALACE and THE THAI HOUSE. Then there is THE GOLDEN
GUINEA at **Redcliffe** *and THE TOPPER at* **St Georges**. *Something*
for everyones taste and pockets here.

The harbour is a two and a half mile stretch of calm, deep waterway
right in the heart of the city, the legacy of Bristol's maritime past. No
longer is it one of the world's busiest harbours. Those days have gone
but what has emerged is an imaginatively transformed major leisure and
recreation centre. Where once John Cabot departed to discover North
America there are now shops, museums, cinemas, and arts centres, an
exhibition centre, pubs and restaurants. It is lively and a fun place to be.

One of my favourite ways of seeing it is to take one of Bristol Ferry
Boats from **St Augustines Reach**. *It stops at fourteen landing stages*
and allows you a chance to sit back and take in much that you might
otherwise miss. At the head of the Reach is one of Bristol's best loved
landmarks, NEPTUNE'S STATUE. There are some picturesque dock
cottages dating from 1831 with a popular pub, THE NOVA SCOTIA.
Another pub, THE OSTRICH, at **Bathurst Basin**, *is a fine 18th-*
century building and on a balmy day there is nothing pleasanter than
sitting outside having a drink. THE FAIRBAIRN STEAM CRANE,
built in 1875 is now a Scheduled Ancient Monument under the control
of the City Museum. Warehouses have been developed into housing. At

Merchants Landing *two original warehouses have been rebuilt in the Bristol Byzantine style. THE ARNOLFINI contemporary arts complex is in St Augustine's Reach on the corner of Prince Street.*

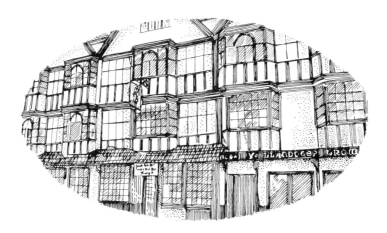

The Llandoger Trow Pub

Further down the Reach, THE MARITIME HERITAGE CENTRE houses a fine collection of artifacts and models explaining the history of shipbuilding in Bristol from medieval times to the present day. Isambard Kindom Brunel's S.S. GREAT BRITAIN, the first ship to be built of iron and driven by a screw propeller is one of the main attractions in Bristol. Occasionally at weekends you will see the restored locomotive HENBURY steaming along from THE INDUSTRIAL MUSEUM to the S.S. Great Britain. Permanently moored in the **Floating Harbour** going towards Castle Park is a Lightship which once gave warning to seafarers in the North Sea. It plays a very different role today as a pub and restaurant moored in the Welsh Back. From here you can see THE LLANDOGER TROW one of Bristol's oldest and most famous inns, believed to have been the model for the 'Admiral Benbow' in R.L. Stevenson's Treasure Island. Bristol Bridge stands on the site of the original Saxon structure that gave the city its name 'Bridgstow – the place of the bridge'.

Can you equate philanthropy with the slave-trade? Edward Colston, Bristol's greatest benefactor, found no difficulty in it. He was a bigoted High Churchman who made his money from the slave trade and gave vast sums of money to charities that still survive today. In Bristol you cannot escape his name, there are schools, almshouses, Colston Hall, renowned for its concerts, Colston Avenue where he is remembered in a great bronze showing him leaning on a cane, and Colston Parade. He laid down stringent conditions as to where his money went. Only Anglicans for example could attend his schools. Bristol certainly gained but I wonder if you can buy your way into the next world with this sort of benevolence?

Whilst the church is on my mind let me tell you something about some of the most beautiful churches in the country. Elizabeth I certainly thought so when she saw ST MARY, **Redcliffe**, in 1574. She described it as 'the fairest, goodliest and most famous parish church in England'. It contains among its many memorable features a tomb to the church cat, who was resident from 1912-27. The church was built between the early 13th century and the 15th century on the Avon's red cliffs, when Redcliffe was inhabited by wealthy merchants. If you think the exterior is magnificent you will find the interior equally inspiring. Arches and pillars soar in exquisite slenderness and grace to the ribbed vaults, which are studded with more than 1,200 bosses, each different. These were covered in pure gold when in 1740 Bristol women gave their jewellery for melting down.

Municipal quarter-jacks

The American Chapel contains a ship's figurehead of Elizabeth I, and many fragments of medieval glass make up a window. The tomb of William Penn senior is in the South transept. It was his son, William, who founded Pennsylvania. The whale rib brought back by the Cabots, who sailed from Redcliffe Harbour in 1497 and discovered Newfoundland, is under the tower. The Royal Arms of Charles II are gorgeously coloured and framed. There are two effigies of William Canynges, a vastly wealthy merchant, who restored the church after the spire was struck by lightning in 1446 and for some reason there is the tombstone of his cook, with knife and colander on it. This is not a church just to behold in awe. It is a place to worship and to enjoy the many concerts and recitals particularly in July when it is the setting for the annual music festival.

In **Broad Street**, in the heart of the city is Christ Church with St Ewen which was rebuilt in 1791 by Bristol architect, William Paty. The dragon vane on the spire was brought from the earlier church as well as the Quarter Jacks of 1728, the Renatus Harris organ and fine case, and the Lord Mayor's sword rest. It is quite lovely with a sublime white and gold domed interior influenced by Wren.

All Saints church in **Corn Street**, is partially Norman and part Perpendicular. There are memorials to the Colston family. Rysbrack designed that to Edward Colston. It shows him as a reclining figure, his thoughts, no doubt, working out how he could perform more philanthropic deeds.

The splendid Cathedral on **College Green** contains many beautiful and historic features, including a fine Norman Chapter House. The early English Lady Chapel is one of the most tranquil places in the whole of Bristol and the unique 14th-century choir contains misericords and a 19th-century nave.

All these churches are open daily, from 8am-6pm, for worship, quiet prayer or the sheer joy of revelling in their magnificence.

Bristol's University is respected throughout the world and many of its fine buildings are very close to the **City Centre**. This no doubt helps to boost the thriving entertainment industry. You can almost always be sure of finding good theatre.

Old and new mix together with remarkable harmony. The city suffered considerably from bombing in World War II and even today vast new building projects are still removing traces of bombed sites. The old part contains much of the business world. WOOD'S EXCHANGE stands on or near the site of the medieval Tolzey, a low roofed arcade *along the wall of All Saints. It was here that merchants strolled and chatted and carried out their business in a sociable manner. They were good at bargaining and when the deal had been struck, they would pay their money 'on the nail', that is one of the squat bronze pillars still standing outside the Exchange. There are several small enchanting streets that hide away immediately behind the hustle and bustle of Broad Street. There are side alleys and courts, like Tailors' Court. Behind the Hippodrome are more lanes leading to streets that house the legal profession in buildings which once must have been delightful homes. One of the most picturesque places must be **Christmas Street** and **Christmas Steps**, its steep slopes bordered by a wealth of interesting small shops. At the top of the steps an Antique Market brings together a cluster of stalls each offering different treasures of the past. **Frogmore Street** has the 17th-century Hatchet Inn, once part of a row. Then there is **Orchard Street** which has to be the loveliest Georgian Street in Bristol.*

You need time to explore Bristol and sometimes to learn about its past before you start seeking out its treasures. It may be advisable to take advantage of the many very good Museums. The CITY MUSEUM AND ART GALLERY is the major museum of the area with displays representing applied art, fine art, oriental art, archaeology, geology and natural history. It has an outstanding collection of European ceramics and glass, and particularly noteworthy are the galleries of archaeology and natural history. Open 10am-5pm except Sundays.

*THE GEORGIAN HOUSE, just off **Park Street**, built 1789-91, is fully furnished in the elegant style of the period and is maintained as a museum. Open 10-1pm 2-5pm. Closed Sundays.*

The LORD MAYOR'S CHAPEL is all that remains above ground of the medieval Hospital of the Gaunts founded in 1220. The interior with its 16th-century stained glass windows and the Poyntz chapel with its Spanish floor tiles and fan vaulted ceiling, is well worth seeing. Open 10am-12noon and 1pm-4pm, closed on Fridays.

Backing onto The Lord Mayors Chapel in Park Street is HARVEY'S WINE MUSEUM housed in the 13th-century cellars of the Gaunt's Hospital. This unique place contains displays of antique cork-screws, bottles, decanters, drinking glasses, etc. It is normally open to the public by appointment only. However, visitors over 18 are welcome on Friday mornings without prior appointment.

*Working your way towards **Broadmead** Shopping Centre, an exciting place with a history of its own, you will spot ST NICHOLAS CHURCH on the corner of **Baldwin** and **St Nicholas Street**. This is* no longer used as a church but houses instead displays of Bristol topographical watercolours, church plate and furnishings, and a brass rubbing centre. There is also an exhibition of archaeological finds which explains the early history of the city. Open 10am-5pm. Closed on Sundays.

Having worked your way round to Broadmead you will see that there is still considerable building taking place. It is an adventurous project which has caused not a few ruffled feathers as old has been demolished to make way for new. It contains every major store and hundreds of smaller shops, many of them now housed in The Galleries. It is almost pedestrianised which makes it a joy in which to shop or browse. In the midst of newness is John Wesley's Chapel, the famous New Room, which was the first Methodist church in the world. Of particular interest is the double-decked pulpit from which Wesley preached. Outside in the courtyard is a fine bronze equestrian statue of John Wesley. It is no distance from there to QUAKERS' FRIAR which is part of the domestic buildings of the Dominican Friary founded in 1227. Today, part of the building houses the Planning Exhibition which also contains the Bristol Historic Tapestry – a pictorial description of the city's history. The adjoining 18th-century building is the former Rosemary Street Friends Meeting house.

There is so much to see and take in that by now you may well have got mental indigestion. There are many pleasing places away from the centre. **Clifton** with its Downs, a 400 acres green expanse, and wonderful houses, particularly the terrace of Regency houses known as The Paragon where the fronts are concave and the porches curve the other way, with convex double doors. Clifton is elegant and gracious and almost like a village, yet it is a place of many contrasts. Architects must have had a sense of theatre when they built Royal York Crescent and Windsor Terrace on its cliff over the Gorge. In Canynge Square there are dainty balconied houses and rows of very squat, rather boring Victorian villas. It has some excellent restaurants and delightful pubs and wine bars. If you still have the energy you can carry on and visit BRISTOL ZOO on the downs. One of the foremost in the country it is a super place to visit. Go far enough and you will come to Brunel's graceful and miraculous Suspension Bridge which looks right up the Avon Gorge.

To reach another great open expanse, **Durdham Downs**, you must go through **Horfield**, which is more famous today for its prison than anything else but it is worth stopping there to visit THE GANGES, an Indian restaurant with style and first class food. The journey will take you up **Blackboy Hill** which has restaurants of every nationality. From the Downs you get the most magnificent views of the Gorge. There *are vantage points and seats where you can sit to take in this extraordinary sight.*

The preservation of the ageless and spacious Downs truly 'from time immemorial' to this crowded century, is an achievement of which Bristol can be rightly proud. I wonder how many people stop to think of their turbulent past however, as they stroll or sit amidst their beauty. For many years they became the haunt of petty thieves, highwaymen who never seem to have achieved any 'gentlemanly' fame, and turbulent gangs of colliers from Kingswood. At the beginning of the 18th century the Kingswood miners, made desperate by poverty and the appalling conditions in which they lived and worked, were the cause of many disturbances around Bristol. There were constant riots which troops were called out to disperse but no sooner had the soldiers gone than the rioters were back again. They continued to terrorise the Downs until well after 1730.

Clifton Suspension Bridge

As Bristol grew, encompassing the villages of Clifton, Westbury and others, the Downs became the favourite spot for residents of Clifton to promenade and take the air. It was not only the natural beauty they sought but recreation and amusement. The OSTRICH INN on **Durdham Down** became one of the most fashionable and popular meeting places in Bristol in the second half of the 18th century. For the benefit of latecomers, at a time when there were no street lamps, the inn-keeper erected lamps on the Downs and lit them nightly during the *winter. Part of the accepted routine for visitors to Hotwells Spa was that they should go riding on the Downs and take breakfast at the Ostrich.*

There were sporting events too. Durdham Down Races were very popular. The meeting would last two days with probably three races a day. Boxing, wrestling and cockfighting contests were held from time to time. May Day revels and fancy dress processions brought the crowds out from the surrounding area. Among the less boisterous activities were cricket matches. What is now THE OBSERVATORY was once a windmill but an artist, Mr West, who was skilled in the construction of telescopes, was allowed to rent the site for a nominal rent. He built one vast telescope, twenty-one feet in focal length which was elevated to the top of the building. It was surrounded by a balcony and visitors were invited to see 'one of the most extensive and beautiful panoramic views in the kingdom'. You still can and it is still wonderful, placed high on the cliff top above the gorge. You can also get refreshments there.

Westbury-on-Trym *once was an attractive village on the out-skirts of Bristol but that has long since ceased. It is now known simply as Westbury and very much part of the city. That does not stop it having two interesting places in which to eat and drink. THE BRITISH RAJ offers one of the best curries in the city and THE VICTORIA, a friendly, welcoming establishment in which good food is just a part of what they have to offer.*

It was inevitable that the ever growing Bristol would need dormitory areas and that is what it has found in places like Failand, Clevedon and Portishead. It is so easy to reach these places now. The cars pour out across the suspension bridge in the evening to commuterdom. Many go on to **Clevedon**, *a charming Victorian resort which has a pier. It is more than worth driving out to visit. On summer evenings the people of Clevedon can look through their windows and see the evening sunlight dancing on the panes of the houses across the Channel in Newport. Clevedon is also blessed by ALEXANDRAS, a delightful eating house. It is also worth visiting CLEVEDON CRAFT CENTRE with its 12 studios and a tea-room in the outbuildings of the 17th-century farm which was once part of Clevedon Court. There is no admission charge and car parking is free. Open throughout the year 11am-5pm. Slightly nearer the city is* **Portishead** *where a drink in THE POACHER would not go amiss on any evening.*

Go further south and you come to Bristol's favourite seaside place, **Weston-Super-Mare** *where you can still take donkey rides on the immense, rather muddy sands. As a child I used to think that Flat Holm and Steep Holm, not far from the shore, were two partly submerged* whales. It was a bitter disappointment when I discovered they were just rather curious shaped small islands sticking out of the sea! Weston will provide anyone looking for fun, with a great time. It has endless amusement parks, restaurants, pubs, a small theatre and cinema. Great for a family holiday if you have youngsters. Situated at the southern end of the Marine Parade is the WESTON MINIATURE RAILWAY which runs for over half a mile around an excellent 18 hole putting course and along the beach lawns, overlooking the sea. The railway and putting course are open Easter week, weekends until spring bank holiday, then daily until late September.

The TROPICANA PLEASURE BEACH is an exciting leisure complex which offers fun for all the family throughout the day. There is a heated surf pool with wave machine and giant water chutes, a shallow children's lagoon and a Rainbow Pool for toddlers. There is acres of room for sunbathing and fast food catering in the Hungry Giant and a licensed bar.

In Burlington Street you will find the award winning WOODSPRING MUSEUM. It is a fascinating place. The main courtyard is adorned with palm trees and a fountain and is surrounded by a collection of exhibits depicting a Victorian seaside holiday. Other impressive features include a nature gallery, exhibits of local industry and archaeology, Mendip minerals and mining, an old chemist's shop and a display of early bicycles. Frequent exhibitions are also staged on specific themes.

CLARA'S COTTAGE, a restored Weston seaside landlady's lodging of the 1890's also includes the Peggy Nisbet doll collection. Open daily except Sundays from 10am-5pm. Admission free.

I have to admit that it is the centre of Bristol and Clifton that I find most rewarding. It is a never ending journey of discovery but one thing I have learnt in my travels is that it pays to go and explore the less well publicised places, for it is there you frequently come upon the most unexpected treasures.

MULLIGAN'S FISH RESTAURANT

Restaurant

43 College Green,
Bristol BS1 5SH
Tel: (0272) 226460

Surrounded by restaurants and wine bars of all nationalities, Mulligan's Fish & Chip Restaurant, Oyster Bar & Charcoal Grill is definitely different. Your first introduction to it will be a vast pool in the window full of water plants. Inside it is a spacious welcoming bar where you can drink before going further into the restaurant. Whilst there is plenty of room Mulligans still remains an intimate place.

The specialities of the house are traditional English Fish and Chips, and speciality dishes such as Oysters, Lobsters and Crab. The menu, however, caters for all tastes and palates. Only the finest fish and seafood is used and if anything is not up to standard or unavailable in the market daily, it will not appear on the menu. You will notice that there is a Blackboard which states what items are unavailable. It also tells you what daily specialities have been produced. The staff are all young and friendly and obviously enjoy the ambience of Mulligans.

For non-fish lovers, Mulligan's offers various dishes from their Charcoal Grill, for example: succulent Sirloin steaks either simply grilled or 'Marchand du Vin' (red wine and shallot sauce), spiced chicken, and the homely sausage and mash. The starters are tempting with a good selection of puddings and sweets, followed by a cheese board. Mulligans is fun, the food is excellent and the price is fair.

USEFUL INFORMATION

OPEN: Mon-Sun: 12-2.15pm
(last orders) Eve: 5.30-10.45pm
Sun: 5.30-10.30pm
CHILDREN: Welcome to eat
CREDIT CARDS: Visa/Access
LICENSED: Full Licence
GARDEN: No

RESTAURANT: Fish & Seafood a
speciality
BAR FOOD: Not applicable
VEGETARIAN: Yes (not Vegan)
ACCESS FOR THE DISABLED:
Level entrance

THE OLD CASTLE GREEN
Public House

Gloucester Lane,
Old Market, Bristol
Tel: (0272) 550925

Situated in Old Market, which used to be a real street market in the last century, The Old Castle Green is a gem of an old traditional pub with its wooden floor and its polished mahogany bar. These days, Old Market is a thriving business area just a stones throw from Broadmead, which is the main shopping area in Bristol. Park around here and avoid the hassle of central Bristol traffic.

The pub has no juke box, so avoiding that endless racket which spoils many pubs these days. At lunchtime, food service is very fast, straight off the hotplate, so that if your time is limited you can still get your lunch without that agonising wait! Real ales by Marstons are complemented by a full range of spirits and soft drinks, low alchocol drinks and an interesting selection of wines. Food is served all day from 12.15 till 10.30pm.

All the food is daily prepared at the pub from fresh ingredients. The hot dishes of the day, which always include at least two vegetarian dishes, are served with a choice of Basmati rice or Dauphinoise potatoes. Chille con Carne, and Chicken Neapolitan in a creamy sauce made with wine, herbs and tomatoes, are regulars on the menu. Fresh Pasta, Onion Bhajias, Stuffed Naan and huge Salad rolls are also available, together with Landlord David Legg's famous real Indian curries.

USEFUL INFORMATION

OPEN: 11.30-11.00pm Weekends: Closed 3-7.00pm
CHILDREN: Allowed until 8pm
CREDIT CARDS: None taken
LICENSED: Marstons real ales, quality lagers, wines, spirits
GARDEN: Yes, with swings.

RESTAURANT: All one bar, same menu
BAR FOOD: All fresh & varied from £2.00
VEGETARIAN: Yes, at least 2 plus snacks
ACCESS FOR THE DISABLED: Level through garden

Royal Oak House,
55, Prince Street, Bristol

Tel: (0272) 215299

THE RIVERSIDE CAFE
Cafeteria/Sandwich Bar

Prince Street is in one of the most historical parts of Bristol: the city docks. During the beginning of the century it was very famous for its sherry exports and everywhere you will see granite cobble stones, carefully restored historic buildings and, now, many tourist attractions. In the heart of this is the Riverside Cafe which is a busy, friendly cafeteria and sandwich bar.

It is an ideal place to nip in and have an early breakfast, freshly cooked which will give you the energy you will need to explore this fascinating area. The S.S. Great Britain is closeby and you can take boat trips around the docks or take a look at the Maritime and Industrial Museum. Many people find their way to St Nicholas Market or spend time in St Mary's Cathedral. Having done all this then it is time to pop back to the Riverside for a cup of tea or coffee, or if you require something more substantial you will find that there is a good traditional English lunch served every day at an extremely reasonable price. Sandwiches are the great speciality of this spotlessly clean establishment. The bread is always fresh and the fillings are full of variety. The service is fast and friendly and everything is value for money.

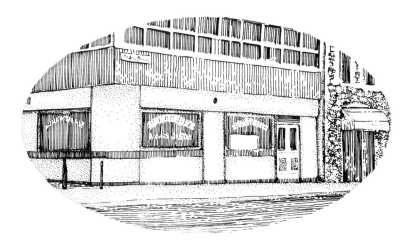

USEFUL INFORMATION

OPEN: Mon-Fri 7.30am-3.20pm
CHILDREN: Welcome
CREDIT CARDS: No. Luncheon
vouchers taken
LICENSED: No
GARDEN: No

RESTAURANT: Extensive menu
from sandwiches to full meals
BAR FOOD: Not applicable
VEGETARIAN: Yes.
ACCESS FOR THE DISABLED: No

THE CHINA PALACE
Restaurant

18a Baldwin Street,
Bristol BS1 1SE
Tel: (0272) 262719

Open seven days a week, the China Palace has a superb range of 188 Chinese dishes, cooked to perfection by the Cantonese Chef; one of the top three in this country. It is right in the heart of the city just 100 yards from the centre. Closeby is the 2,000 seat Bristol Hippodrome and the historic Theatre Royal, Britain's oldest theatre.

The restaurant is large and luxurious, yet intimate and relaxing with a spacious Mandarin Bar separated from it by a few stairs. Kam Wong, the owner, personally designed all the decor of The China Palace and, drawing on his previous experience as an aircraft engineer, he also designed the unique multi-burner 'Turbo Wok' which is the secret of how so many wonderful Chinese dishes can be cooked so expertly and quickly. The restaurant is air-conditioned, has facilities for dancing and is ideal for parties, receptions and banquets. It has won virtually every award for excellence and has a tradition of organising charity galas with cabaret, live bands and dancing.

Sea food and Chinese fondues are specialities. The most popular dishes of all are aromatic Crispy Peking Duck and sizzling Cantonese Fillet Steak. Dim Sum, the traditional Chinese delicacy is also available 7 days a week, with a specially wide choice on Sundays. The wine list is comprehensive and the choice of de-luxe brandies finishes a meal superbly. Because The China Palace is open from 12 noon-11.30pm every Sunday, lunch can be almost anytime.

USEFUL INFORMATION

OPEN: Mon-Sat:12-2.30pm.
6-11.30pm Sun: 12-11.30pm
CHILDREN: Yes.
CREDIT CARDS: Visa/Access/
Amex
LICENSED: Spirits & Wines and
public entertainment
GARDEN: No. City centre location

RESTAURANT: Gourmet Chinese
traditional dishes
BAR FOOD: Not applicable
VEGETARIAN: Yes. about 8 dishes
ACCESS FOR THE DISABLED: No,
but wide staircase

52, Park Row,
Bristol, BS1 5LH

Tel: (0272) 253079

THE THAI HOUSE
Restaurant

The Thai House is unique and delightful. It has the virtue of being situated close to the Wills Memorial Building and Bristol City Museum as well as being right by the shops of Park Street and Queen's Road. It is equally conveniently sited for business people working in the many nearby offices. Car parking is never a problem because there is plentiful 'on street parking' and an NCP car park just 200 yards along Park Row.

The restaurant occupies the ground floor and garden level of a Victorian building which stood next to the old Princess Victoria Theatre which, sadly, was destroyed in World War II. The bar and the reception area takes the form of a traditional Thai house complete with raftered roof and authentic Thai furnishings. The restaurant is light, spacious, and tastefully decorated with Thai ornaments and wall hangings. The conservatory which lights up the restaurant is full of exotic plants and delicately perfumed with vases of fresh orchids.

Thai food is influenced by Indian and Chinese cuisine but has a unique quality of its own. It is light and delicately flavoured and beautifully presented. To aid the uninitiated there are a range of suggested menus to help you choose and get the balance right. Once you have made your selection, assisted by the staff who all come from Thailand, renowned for its hospitality, you can relax in the comfortable surroundings. It is the perfect place for lunch or evening meals and a superb venue for those who want to entertain business clients or friends. The Thai House does not open on Sundays.

USEFUL INFORMATION

OPEN: Mon-Sat: 12-2.30pm. 6.30 – Last orders 11-15pm
CHILDREN: Permitted at anytime
CREDIT CARDS: Visa/Access/ Diners/Amex
LICENSED: Full Licence
GARDEN: No

RESTAURANT: Authentic Thai cuisine. Delicate, spicy, light & delicious
BAR FOOD: Not applicable
VEGETARIAN: Special menu + 2 starters, 10 main courses
ACCESS FOR THE DISABLED: Too many stairs

ALEXANDRA'S RESTAURANT
Restaurant

The Old Market Hall,
Alexandra Road,
Clevedon, Avon

Tel: (0272) 872093

After the hustle and bustle of Bristol nearby Clevedon is a small, quiet seaside town with a great deal of charm. In its midst is the Old Market Hall which attracts many people because it is quite unlike any other market. Certainly you will not find a market hall as pretty anywhere else in the county. Built in 1867 it is still used for its original purpose – the buying and selling of wares. At the time the hall was intended to stop the nuisance of traders hauling their wares around the town. But it has served other functions like a reception for the grand opening of Clevedon Pier.

In 1980 the market was threatened with demolition due to local government cuts but was saved by a local businessman who spent thousands of pounds restoring it. It is a hive of industry. Stallholders set up their booths on the ancient flagstone floors and the market has a carefully selected number of exclusive shops. It is fascinating but the picture would not be complete without Alexandra's Restaurant, a place to enjoy delicious food, be looked after by friendly welcoming staff and sit back to savour all that you have seen and are about to eat. The food is all home-made, with some of the lightest pastry you will ever taste. Daily specials, cream teas and many other traditional English meals are available. Betty O'Connor, the proprietor, has ensured that Alexandra's is not to be missed.

USEFUL INFORMATION

OPEN: Mon-Sat: 9.30am-5.00pm
CHILDREN: Very welcome
CREDIT CARDS: None taken
LICENSED: Wines, beers & lagers
GARDEN: Patio with tables outside

RESTAURANT: Wholesome, good value food
BAR FOOD: Not applicable
VEGETARIAN: Several dishes
ACCESS FOR THE DISABLED: Level entrance

368. Gloucester Road,
Horfield, Bristol
Tel: (0272) 245234/428505

THE GANGES
Restaurant

On the main A38, just 2 miles from the City Centre, is a very popular Indian Restaurant, The Ganges. Owned by Mr Chowdhury, who opened it first in 1981, it has an established reputation for good Indian food served in a room that is decorated to give the true feeling of Eastern authenticity. There are cosy, intimate alcoves where one can dine or lunch with a degree of privacy and upstairs there is a second dining room known as 'Biplob'. Both are rich in colour; the use of red, green and gold gives an aura of splendour and graciousness.

You will find the staff are trained to a high standard of efficiency, which includes a degree of friendliness and helpfulness which is so important if you are to get the best out of an Indian meal. Knowing what to choose is not always easy and you will find the waiters are more than ready to assist. Whatever your final decision is, it will come to table beautifully presented.

The menu has a wide range of dishes from which to choose. Some of them quite unusual like Chicken Jaal, Panir Gisht, Rezala and Shaslik. You need not be afraid that everything will be too hot for you; you can choose, and will be advised to select, dishes that will be right for your palate. There are always five dishes for vegetarians and at no time are frozen vegetables ever used. It all adds up to a restaurant offering the highest standard of food and service.

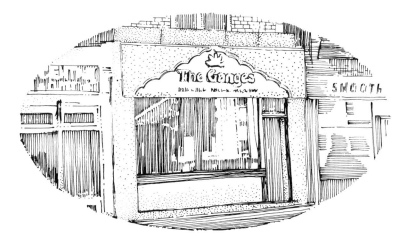

USEFUL INFORMATION

OPEN: 12-2.30pm, 6-11.30pm daily
CHILDREN: Welcome
CREDIT CARDS: Amex/Diners/
Visa/Mastercard
LICENSED: High quality beers &
wines including Indian
GARDEN: No.

RESTAURANT: High quality Indian
dishes
BAR FOOD: Not applicable
VEGETARIAN: 5 dishes
ACCESS FOR THE DISABLED: Yes

THE BELL INN

Public House

21, Alfred Place,
Kingsdown, Bristol
Tel: (0272) 215398

Two lively, professional women, Alison Gunn Robson and Anna Luke, welcome you at The Bell, in one of the earliest of Bristol's villages, Kingsdown. Located on the cliffs above the city centre it was once the haunt of smugglers. Today it is haunted by a cosmopolitan clientele described by Alison and Anna as a 'heady mix of Peer and Pauper which makes for interesting conversation at the bar'. How true; it is the most entertaining place to be.

The Bell was not built as a pub but as two Victorian terraced houses which have lent themselves beautifully to the conversion. There is nothing pretentious about it but it does have a wonderful atmosphere. Most of their customers are regulars who are never averse to welcoming strangers into their midst. So often today a pub has lost its traditional purpose as a meeting place. No one could ever say that about The Bell. It is the sort of place that you will wish you could transport back to your own home town.

The food lives up to the standard of The Bell. Every dish is home-made; it does not come out of a tin or freezer plastic! The dishes are simple ones: frequently, mouth-watering casseroles of Pork Beef or Lamb. There is an excellent Sausage and Bean Hot Pot, a tantalising Chilli and common or garden Faggots and Peas. Fish plays an important part on the menu and so do vegetarian dishes. It is excellent value for money.

USEFUL INFORMATION

OPEN: 12-3.00pm. 5.30-11.00pm,
Sat:12-11.00pm
CHILDREN: No
CREDIT CARDS: Cheques with
Bankers cards
LICENSED: 3 Real Ales, 3 Lagers,
good selection wines, all spirits
GARDEN: None

RESTAURANT: Not applicable
BAR FOOD: Exceptional Quality
Menu
VEGETARIAN: 2 dishes + fish
ACCESS FOR THE DISABLED:
Level entrance

106, High Street,
Portishead, Bristol
Tel: (0272) 844002

THE POACHER
Public House

Portishead has grown from a village into a town but still has just one main street, the High Street, with The Poacher in the centre. It is an attractive, grey stone building with a large car park and frontage, set in the midst of shops and offices. The first license was granted in 1683 when it was known as the Blew Anchor. During the 1720's, a widow lady, Mary Whitwood, ran the pub and had stocks and a whipping post outside with which to dispense justice! The pub has changed its name several times: in 1850 it became the Gordon Arms, to appease the local squire; a little later it was re-named the Anchor, and became The Poacher 14 years ago, some 9 years before the present landlord, Mr Hazelton, and his wife took over.

The Hazeltons are a convivial couple whose aim has always been to make people welcome. They have achieved a wonderful atmosphere which not only attracts customers but their caring attitude has meant also, that the staff have stayed with them over the years.

The food is excellent. There are about thirty home made dishes from which to choose, including many favourites such as: Somerset Chicken in Cider, Braised Steak and Onions, Beef Stew and Dumplings, Pork Hot Pot, and Lamb Stew. In addition to these there is a range of fish, meat and vegetarian dishes, as well as freshly made sandwiches, Ploughmans lunches and hot and cold sweets. The quality is first class and super value for money.

USEFUL INFORMATION

OPEN: 11-2.30pm 6-11.00pm
CHILDREN: Not allowed
CREDIT CARDS: None taken
LICENSED: Full Licence
GARDEN: None

RESTAURANT: Not applicable
BAR FOOD: 30+ home-made dishes
VEGETARIAN: Cold dishes only
ACCESS FOR THE DISABLED:
Level entrance

THE GOLDEN GUINEA

Public House

Guinea Street,
Redcliffe, Bristol

Tel: (0272) 291109

The Golden Guinea is a very special pub, situated next door to the entrance of the Bristol General Hospital and only 50 yards up the hill from Redcliffe Wharf. It is just minutes from the S.S. Great Britain or Temple Meads, yet, it sits in a quiet Business and Residential area of the city.

The property dates back to 1730 and retains much of its original character. There are no Pool tables or Juke Boxes to destroy the peace but the soft background music of the 50s, 60s and 70s, adds to the atmosphere. To Ron and Sylvia Waterfield, the proprietors, comfort, security, cleanliness and a friendly welcome are all important. Outside there is a south facing patio which is well sheltered and a delightful place to be in the summer with its colourful display of flowers. A lower patio has a purpose built Barbeque. Food naturally plays an important part in the life of the pub and no one coming here will be disappointed with the standard.

Lunchtime meals are basically designed for busy office staff which does not mean that visitors are not welcome. There is a wide variety of curries, steak pies, jacket potatoes, Ploughmans and sandwiches which are all firm favourites, and probably the cheapest in Bristol. Evening meals, which are A La Carte, have to be booked at least 24 hours in advance. The evening and weekend lunch Barbecues are very popular and the pub can cater for up to 60. Sunday lunch is also popular and it is essential to book.

USEFUL INFORMATION

OPEN: 12-3.00pm, 4.30-11.00pm
CHILDREN: Welcome
CREDIT CARDS: None taken
LICENSED: Full Licence
GARDEN: Small front patio. Large rear patio ideal for children.

RESTAURANT: Not applicable
BAR FOOD: Excellent well priced range
VEGETARIAN: 10 various dishes
ACCESS FOR THE DISABLED: No. Stepped entrance

90 Bryants Hill,
St George, Bristol
Tel : (0272) 673326

THE TROOPER
Public House

The proprietors of The Trooper, Philip and Lynne Hunt, knew all about the pub long before they became mine hosts; they were regulars. In those days it had a friendly atmosphere which Philip and Lynne have continued and in the ten months that they have been here they have improved the food, nurtured the ale and encouraged the darts, cribbage and local football teams as well as cricket. It is a genuine local pub which has a strong following and this is increasing steadily because visitors who have never been there before discover that, only six miles from the centre of Bristol, The Trooper is easily reached and offers peace.

It is easy to find on the main road between Bristol and Bath, on the outskirts of Hanham. It is completely detached and has a pleasant garden at the side and a super beer patio at the rear. Car parking is available in front of the pub. You will find that the age of the regulars covers the whole span of drinking years! The keen, competitive sporting links of the pub teams tends to dominate the conversation and it is never dull.

Lynne prides herself on her home-cooked foods, particularly the steak and kidney pie with its mouth watering pastry. She makes a good Cornbeef Hash as well, and many other tempting dishes. You can have chicken, fish, salads, sandwiches and Ploughmans, of course, but you may well be tempted to damage your waistline with the good old fashioned puddings like Spotted Dick or Apple and Sultana Sponge. Whatever you choose you will enjoy and find it is excellent value for money.

USEFUL INFORMATION

OPEN: Mon-Fri: 11-2.30pm
    Sat:11-3.00pm
    Mon-Sat:5.30-11.00pm
    Sun:12-3.00pm 7-10.30pm
CHILDREN: Beer Garden-play area.
    Allowed in lower lounge.
CREDIT CARDS: None taken
LICENSED: Full Licence
GARDEN: Garden & Beer Patio

RESTAURANT: Not applicable
BAR FOOD: Good home-cooked fare
VEGETARIAN: One dish daily
ACCESS FOR THE DISABLED:
    Easy access

THE BRITISH RAJ
Restaurant

1-3 Passage Road,
Westbury-on-Trym, Bristol
Tel: (0272) 507149/500493

Westbury-on-Trym is known locally as the village in the City. It is a picturesque place, 100 yards off the main Bristol and Avonmouth road. It is a mere 15 minutes taxi ride from the centre of Bristol, and with easy access to the Motorway. In the midst of the village is The British Raj, at 1-3 Passage Road, which is quite the friendliest Indian restaurant you will ever visit.

Muleh Ahmed and Todris Ullah are the owners. Their staff are unique inasmuch as they all come from the same village in Bangladesh so that a genuine family atmosphere prevails. Sanur is the chef who is ably assisted by Shahid, whilst Mannaf is the head waiter. The moment you enter the door you will find you are enveloped in the warmth of a true Bangladesh welcome and it will not be long before you are deep in discussion about what you are going to choose from the menu. There are set meals consisting of Sheek Kebab & Murgh Kebab as a starter followed by Chicken and Lamb Bhune as a main course. Mixed Vegetable Curry and Mushroom Bhaji as a vegetable with Pilau Rice followed by a sweet. A Tandoori mixed grill is interesting, consisting of an assortment of Tandoori Chicken, Chicken Tikka, Lamb Sheek and Tandoori King Prawn. You can choose very hot sauces or something quite mild. You can even eat English dishes if need be. Whatever you choose will be carefully and freshly prepared and beautifully presented. It is a good restaurant and certainly value for money.

USEFUL INFORMATION

OPEN: Daily 12noon-2.00pm, 6-11.30pm
CHILDREN: Very welcome
CREDIT CARDS: All cards
LICENSED: Extensive wine list. Beers
GARDEN: No

RESTAURANT: Wide range Indian dishes. English available.
BAR FOOD: Not applicable
VEGETARIAN: Vegetable dishes available
ACCESS FOR THE DISABLED: Yes, plus wide toilet

20, Chock Lane,
Westbury on Trym, Bristol
Tel: (0272) 500441

THE VICTORIA
Public House

Westbury-on-Trym has managed to remain an enchanting village with some super buildings and a fine church, in spite of the fact that it is on the outskirts of Bristol. In the midst of the village is The Victoria, a country pub built in the early 1700s. It was not always a hostelry and in its time has served as the Court house. It would be best to describe this as a family pub, run by Alan and Teresa Adams who seem to have several generations working with them. Their three charming daughters work behind the bar, Father does odd jobs and both Mothers and sister work in the kitchen.

The ease with which you can get to the Victoria, which is only $3^1/_2$ miles from the centre of Bristol, draws many people from the city. Its quiet, sedate setting in the atmosphere of the village gives everyone who comes here a new lease of life. You leave having supped well kept ale, eaten good, home-cooked fare, refreshed in mind and body.

Teresa cooks all the food on the premises. Every day she produces different dishes which can be anything from casseroles to curries. She has a light touch with pastry and a great understanding of sauces. It would be extremely difficult not to find something to please your taste buds. At night she brings out The Victoria's secret weapon – Pizzas! There are a whole variety of fillings and apart from being delicious they are a meal in themselves. If you have not got the time for a meal you will find that the sandwiches, which are freshly cut, an excellent alternative. The Victoria offers warmth, hospitality and value for money.

USEFUL INFORMATION

OPEN: 12-2.30pm 5.30-11.00pm
CHILDREN: When eating
CREDIT CARDS: None taken
LICENSED: Full Licence
GARDEN: Pretty but steep

RESTAURANT: Not applicable
BAR FOOD: Good home-cooked fare
VEGETARIAN: 2 dishes
ACCESS FOR THE DISABLED:
Regrettably none

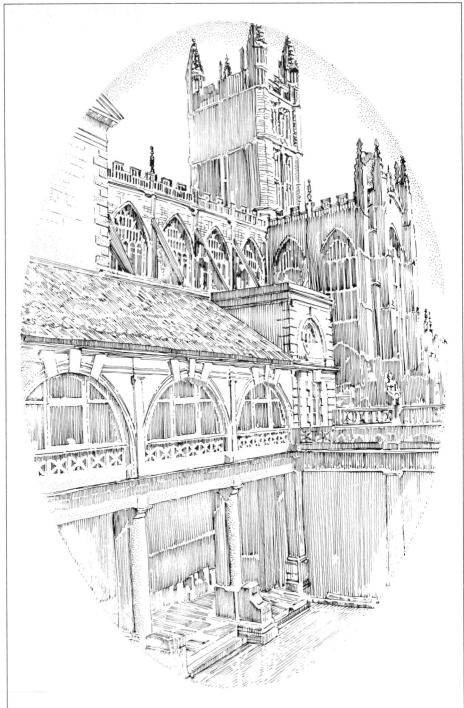

Roman Bath & Abbey

INCLUDES:

"And must I wholly banish hence
These red and golden juices,
And pay my vows to Abstinence,
That pallidest of Muses?"
William Watson

BATH AND AVON

(excluding Bristol)

*The chapter heading puts **Bath** first followed by Avon but I am perverse and intend to keep this jewel in the crown of Britain until last. It is one of the loveliest places in the world, inspite of the planning monstrosities that occurred after World War II. Avon has struggled for years to acquire its own identity but what has always been there, whatever the name of the county, are some charming small towns and villages. **Thornbury** to the immediate north of Bristol is one such a town. Whenever I see it signposted as I drive down the M5 I always think I have reached Bristol, but near as it is, Thornbury has not been encroached by its ever lengthening tentacles.*

Thornbury is a thriving country town and yet has managed to achieve a certain isolation. Yes, it does have traffic problems, but they are home grown ones. The A38 passes to the east of the town, and long before its existence, the old turnpike road avoided it as far back as 1769. It has become a splendid backwater, keeping its old streets and buildings. The main street lay out, which forms the letter Y, by the junction of Castle Street, High Street and the Plane, has not changed since medieval times. In the High Street you will see two fine 18th-century Inns, THE SWAN and THE WHITE LION. There is a well-preserved old Market house and a small Greek temple built in 1839 which was the old Registry Office.

In 1511 Edward Stafford, 3rd Duke of Buckingham, started to build his castle at Thornbury. Ten years later he was beheaded for treason and the Castle appropriated by Henry VIII, who stayed here in 1535 with Anne Boleyn. Mary Tudor lived here for some years and when she became Queen she returned the Castle to the descendants of the late Duke. Today, with its own vineyard and the oldest Tudor garden in England, Thornbury is the only Tudor Castle to be run as an hotel. As you would suspect it is superb, and is rated as one of the 300 best hotels in the world. Quite a reputation to uphold. The resident proprietor, Maurice Taylor, has a fine appreciation of old buildings and cultural heritage. Since he bought it in 1986 it has thrived and been lovingly cared for. You will still find reminders of Buckingham everywhere. A stone carved doorway bears his emblem in relief, the Brecknock Mantle, the Stafford Knot, among other devices. The Knot even appears on the mounting block in the courtyard. Fireplaces too, display the emblems. A wonderful place to eat but it does not profess to be anything other than expensive. Telephone (0454) 418511 for reservations.

*If you decide to stay, lunch or dine in Thornbury Castle you will find it an ideal spot from which to set forth to see **Aust** and **Elberton**. From Roman times Aust was the main ferry route to Chepstow and so to Wales. For the geologist the cliffs, with their various coloured strata and examples of faulting, are wonderful hunting grounds, particularly the Rhaetic bone bed, famous for fossils of prehistoric reptiles.*

Thornbury High Street

Just east of Aust, is Elberton with its church dedicated to St John. Much restoration took place in 1858 and again in 1900 but nothing can mar the beauty of the 14th-century tower. I like the Jacobean manorial box pew, with carved panelling and four holes for inserting sprigs of holly at Christmas time. The manor is right next door, in fact a door from the churchyard leads into the garden of the manor. It is a graceful house built from the 16th-17th century, with three storeys and a cupola on the roof, probably erected to be used for keeping a watchful eye on the labourers working in the fields, for this manor was once a farmhouse.

*Both **Littleton upon Severn** and **Oldbury upon Severn** are a mile or so from the river. In the past they would have been named more accurately for they were villages of the marshland, subject to severe flooding.*

It is very flat round Oldbury but every now and again there are knolls and it is on such knolls that the churches were built to protect them from flooding. This is true of Oldbury church. It is worth a climb up to see it rather more for the view than the church. You will see the Severn Bridge downstream and the great concrete towers of Oldbury Nuclear Power Station in the opposite direction. More to my liking is the view of Chepstow, the Forest of Dean and the foothills of the Welsh Mountains. The church was destroyed by fire in 1897 and rebuilt, but a legend lingers about the first church built there. It was the intention to build it in the village but every night it was destroyed. The villagers consulted an aged hermit, who told them to yoke together two maiden heifers and to build the church where they stopped. The heifers obviously preferred the grazing on the knoll so they stopped there! It is a pretty village with old world cottages and flowering gardens clustering around THE SHIP and THE ANCHOR, two fine hostelries which are named for their connection with the Severn.

Littleton has a little church with a saddle back roof, dedicated to St Mary de Malmesbury. It was virtually demolished in the 19th century because of its state of repair, but several items from the old church remain including the fine Norman font with its chevron design and the two piscinas inserted in the wall by the altar table. Around the foot of the font are tiles from Thornbury Castle.

It is not far down the A38 from Thornbury to **Tockington**, a charming village where, surrounding the green, are old houses and the 300 year old pub, THE SWAN, whose beer is kept cool by a natural spring in the cellar. Another excellent establishment here is THE KITCHEN GARDEN.

The motorways are a blessing in many ways for they allow you to travel more easily from one place to another and do not prevent you from slipping off at various junctions to explore. **Winterbourne** is one such place, although it has really become a part of Bristol today. Its oldest part has managed to stay untouched. In the quiet area around the church are a few cottages, and the adjoining Winterbourne Court Farm. I like to think of Winterbourne when hat-making was a cottage industry and between 1770 and 1870 the whole place flourished with the trade brought to them because fashion dictated the wearing of beaver hats. The church too has a romantic story surrounding a knight whose effigy lies by the north wall. The knight is thought to be Hugo de Sturden who eloped with a fair lady but was a bit of a rogue. He made a pact with the devil in return for certain favours. He agreed that when he died he would not be carried into the church or buried in the churchyard feet or head forward. He managed to cheat even on that and gave instructions for his coffin to be carried in sideways and be buried in the wall. On one wall is a brass which I found fascinating. It is about 1370 and of one of the

Bradestone ladies whose family were lords of the manor. Her dress has pocket holes which show part of the girdle beneath. It is thought to be the oldest brass in the county. A visit to a nice pub, THE WHEATSHEAF, was a pleasant end to my visit here.

Dodington Park

*On the fringe of the Cotswolds there are a number of delight-ful places such as **Marshfield, Dyrham** and **Tormarton** all built of Cotswold stone with its lovely mellowness. Each has its charm and I particularly like Tormarton with its long main street and nice pub, THE PORTCULLIS. There is little development round here because all three villages are within a conservation area. From anyone of them you can set forth to explore places like DODINGTON PARK which is a childrens paradise – and not bad for their elders either. There is a wonderful adventure playground, a carriage museum, and many exhibitions which are either held in the grounds or in Dodington house with its great porticoed front.*

DYRHAM PARK belongs to the National Trust. The west front has glorious views over the countryside towards Bristol. It is a delightful building crowned with a balustrade and has a courtyard terrace flanked by one-storey wings, one of which leads to the medieval village church. You will find the interior much influenced by the Dutch fashions. It is lovely and I do not know which is more beautiful, the magnificent 18th-century park with groves and clumps of beeches, chestnuts and cedars, or the house. The little village clusters round the church and the walled grounds of the manor house.

The name **Badminton** must be familiar to anyone who enjoys equestrian events. BADMINTON PARK, the seat of the Duke of Beaufort, is where the famous Horse trials are held in April frequently attended by members of the Royal Family. It is only a little to the north of Sodbury and surrounded by the most beautiful countryside. The house, which is one of the great stately homes of England, was built for the 3rd Marquess of Worcester who became the first Duke of Beaufort. It was enlarged somewhere in the mid 17th century by William Kent who also designed Worcester Lodge, a gateway on the northern boundary of the park. It is here that the Beaufort Hunt meet on Boxing Day morning. A sight worth seeing, you will always find a large number of people there to enjoy the spectacle and watch the riders and hounds depart.

Nothing to do with horses, but with another game, is the story that Badminton was invented here. It was quite usual for the family of a former duke to play tennis in the entrance hall causing damage to the many valuable pictures, so a new version using a shuttlecock instead of a hard tennis ball was tried out and the game of badminton came into being.

I meant to get onto the A46 which would take me to Bath but somehow I missed it and found myself on the A429 which led me via Chippenham to Bath, and en route I found a turning off to **Hinton Dyrham** where I stopped to get a drink and some food at THE BULL INN. It was an unexpected pleasure and I was not sorry to have missed my way. I would not like you to miss the A46 route from the M4 to Bath though because it gives you sight of some of the most wonderful countryside in Avon, the tree lined hills alternate with lush fields and just as you think you have seen something wondrous it is capped by something even more beautiful around another corner.

To the west of Bath is the **Chew Valley** with its many delightful villages but dominated by the great reservoir, **Chew Valley Lake**. It is an amazing place with ten miles of shore and some wonderful views. It is a mecca for many different enthusiasts. People come here to sail, to fish; the birdwatchers are in their element studying the great variety of bird life to be found here. Many people come, I suspect, as I do just to enjoy its great beauty and to take a stroll. It is one of mans great achievements which whilst supplying water to Bristol, its main purpose, annually gives great pleasure to so many.

*If you want a good place to eat inexpensively whilst you are in this area then THE RED LION at **Bishop Sutton** is the answer. The village is not very interesting. It was once a mining village but is now a commuter residential area for Bath and Bristol. Making my way back towards Bath I went through **Midsomer Norton** which always disappoints me. I am attracted by the romanticism of the name but like Bishop Sutton it has mining origins and little beauty. Indeed the next stop **Radstock** is exactly the same but the latter is redeemed by a good pub THE FROMEWAY.*

Bath's Pultney Bridge

*And so to **Bath**. It is always with a certain amount of impatience and eager anticipation that I seek out this incomparable city. I prefer to behave in the manner of an ostrich and bury my head in the sand when it comes to the outskirts or the 'new' Bath which arose because of indifferent planning. Thankfully, Georgian Bath still remains. It is not individual buildings that make this city so wonderful but the whole architectural assembly. Take a walk down through Laura Place looking at the houses in which society used to dwell in its heyday when Bath was a fashionable watering place, cross Argyle Street and so to Pulteneny Bridge which spans the Avon. You could be forgiven for thinking you were in Florence as you cross this enchanting bridge which has small shops on either side of it not unlike the Ponte Vecchio. The Abbey must come on your list of places to see. It is probably the most beautiful place* *in the city. There is more glass than stone in the walls which fill it with light.*

There are Museums galore and each has something special to offer. The Pump and Assembly Rooms have been the centre of social life since the early 18th century. The PUMP ROOM was originally built for serious medicinal purposes. Doctors, led by Dr William Oliver, (the creator of the Bath Oliver biscuit) felt that invalids would benefit if they drank Bath's mineral waters together. A worthy thought but Beau Nash, the city's Master of Ceremonies, had other ideas. He saw that a Pump Room could be useful as a social centre and so he hired musicians to play there. Soon visitors flocked there every morning to meet their friends, frequently returning in the afternoon to take tea. Today you can still drink the waters and have coffee as well.

The ASSEMBLY ROOMS have always been available for parties, and are still so today as well as for concerts, antique fairs and even tea dances. In the basement there is the Museum of Costume.

No. 1 ROYAL CRESCENT cannot really be called a museum or a private house but well worth visiting. In the 18th century it was used as a lodging house for fashionable people staying in Bath for the season. The Bath Preservation Trust has restored the house which it was given by the late Bernard Caber. They have restored it almost to its 18th century condition, with Georgian furniture, paintings and china. One odd thing about all these houses in the Royal Crescent is that, when they were built, they had not kitchens in the main building – servants brought food from outhouses or elsewhere.

Like Bristol, Bath has a lot of water about. Canal or river trips are very rewarding. From Pulteney Weir, three boats, the Avon Vanity, the George Washington and the Scenic I make the trip up river to Bathampton Weir and back, giving you a wonderful riverside view of the city. The Kennet and Avon Canal have fully restored the canal from Bath to Caen Hill at Devizes and you can take trips in narrowboats or even a leisurely three hour evening cruise from Sydney Wharf on the John Rennie, which includes a three course dinner en route.

Where to eat? There are many excellent places. SALLY LUNN'S HOUSE, of course, which has been a popular meeting place since the days of Beau Nash. The giant brioche muffins are named after the 17th-century Hugenot pastrycook. It is believed that the buns were much older though and were possibly baked in Roman times. Excavations in the cellar show that in 200AD the site was a mansion where food was prepared and eaten. One of the prettiest places in summer is THE MOON AND SIXPENCE, off Broad Street, which has a delightful courtyard in which in summer you eat the delectable salads which are the speciality. THE GREEN PARK BRASSERIE, situated in a restored station building, will delight steam railway enthusiasts and give them a value for money lunch at the same time. DENMUTH'S COFFEE HOUSE has three floors, two of which are dedicated to healthy eating, a plus for vegetarians. The Pump Room is open all day too for lunches and teas. THE DOWER HOUSE RESTAURANT at the Royal Crescent Hotel and THE HOLE IN THE WALL have well deserved reputations for culinary excellence which will make the rather hefty bills acceptable. One of my favourites is CLARET'S RESTAURANT AND WINE BAR in Kingsmead Square which has its being in four vaults under a lovely Georgian Terrace. The city has some excellent Asian and Oriental restaurants of which THE RAJPOOT TANDOORI in Argyle Street is my favourite.

*If you feel like a short run outside Bath then I can recommend THE OAKHILL INN at **Oakhill** or THE GEORGE AND DRAGON at **Batheaston**, both offer good food and hospitality and the bill will not make you reach for the valium!*

THE RAJPOOT

Restaurant

Rajpoot House,
4, Argyle Street, Bath, Avon
Tel: (0225) 466833/464758

Close to Pulteney Bridge and Pulteney Street in the centre of Bath is The Rajpoot Restaurant at 4, Argyle Street. This is an internationally known establishment where people come not only to eat the superb food but also to become acquainted with the true spirit of India. You are greeted by a doorman in Indian costume who takes you to one of the three parts of tbis entrancing restaurant; the Old India, India Cottage or Kamra, all decorated in authentic style.

The owner, Mr Chowdhury, opened the Rajpoot in 1980 and has upgraded everything constantly. The dishes are always checked, frozen food is never used and you will be served by quietly charming Indian staff. It is a great experience. The Rajpoot has established a reputation for serving its own blend of subtly spiced Tandoori and curry dishes, all prepared with great skill and attention to detail. You will find yourself cordially welcome and they will be only too delighted to help with your selection from the extensive menu.

Amongst the many dishes there are several unusual ones including Chicken Jaflang, a curry type of dish using special herbs and spices collected from the hills of Jaflang. Chicken Jhal Noorpuri, cooked with rarely found herbs and green chilli – this dish has to be hot! Rezala, a typical example of a ceremonial dish, cooked with lamb; Kacchi Akhni, a Biriany type of dish using the Rajpoot's blend of subtle herbs and spices, served with a small bowl of sauce, and many others including Vegetarian dishes. If you have room at the end of your main course, there are also some exotic and unusual Indian sweets.

USEFUL INFORMATION

OPEN: 12-2.30pm. 6-11.00pm Fri & Sat: until 11.30pm
CHILDREN: Welcome
CREDIT CARDS: Amex/Diners/ Visa/Mastercard
LICENSED: From Indian lager & wine to all high quality wines & beers
GARDEN: No.

RESTAURANT: Superb, authentic & unusual dishes
BAR FOOD: Not applicable
VEGETARIAN: 4 dishes
ACCESS FOR THE DISABLED: Access by arrangement

Sutton Hill Road,
Bishops Sutton, Bristol, Avon

Tel: Chew Magna 332689

THE RED LION
Public House

This is a traditional village pub on the main A368, situated in the Chew valley, an area of outstanding natural beauty. It is only a short walk from The Red Lion to the popular Chew Valley Lake which is famous for trout fishing and scenic walks. It is also within easy reach of Bath, Wells, Bristol and Weston-Super-Mare.

Philip and Susan Blenkiron are the hosts of this appealing 19th-century establishment which has retained that special unspoilt village character. Apart from the excellent beer and food, of particular interest are the old photographs which tell the story of the village history quite graphically, with special reference to the local mines and mill. The interest that the Blenkirons take in the local history rubs off on their staff who are always willing to talk to visitors and to help them plan a day out in the area. It is without doubt one of the nicest hostelries in this part of Avon.

The menu spoils you for choice. There are the house specialities amongst which is Chew Valley Trout, home cooked traditional English fare and some equally good continental dishes. Every day there is a tempting 'Dish of the Day' and on Wednesdays and Fridays you will find a special Pensioners Lunch. Vegetarians are not forgotten; there are always at least three tasty dishes available. Children are catered for too, both with their own menu and the safe walled garden where there is a good variety of play equipment.

USEFUL INFORMATION

OPEN: Mon-Fri: 11.30-2.30pm
6-11.00pm Sat:11.30-3.00pm
Sun:12-3.00pm. 7-10.30pm
CHILDREN: Welcome to eat inside
CREDIT CARDS: None taken
LICENSED: Full Licence
GARDEN: Safe, walled garden.
B.B.Que area. Patio, tables for
eating out, children play
equipment

RESTAURANT: Not applicable
BAR FOOD: Extensive.Home-cooked
English fare. Continental &
Vegetarian dishes
VEGETARIAN: 3 dishes daily
ACCESS FOR THE DISABLED:
Level entrance

THE BULL INN
Public House

Hinton Dyrham,
Nr Chippenham, Avon
Tel: (0275 82) 2332

The first thing that will strike you about The Bull Inn is the ample car parking space and the huge garden with its terrace. Here in the summer it is a delightful place to be. Meals can be taken outside which is a boon for parents. Dining on cooler days within the bars of the pub is just as pleasant. The Bacons are mine hosts and their friendly outgoing personalities ensure everyone, whether they are regular locals or visitors, enjoy The Bull. It is comfortably furnished but has that well worn look which makes you feel at ease.

At the bar you will find the locals enjoying their pint of well kept ale and whilst they are jealous of what they consider to be their territory, they do not make outsiders feel unwanted which is one of the failings of many village hostelries. The trade at The Bull comes from an ever widening area as its reputation spreads and people regularly return. At Christmas time its popularity is only too evident and is much in demand for staff parties.

In the restaurant steaks are the speciality of the house. Simply served but cooked just in the way that you request, with other favourite, traditional choices of different fare should you prefer. In the Bar the menu offers a wide range from freshly cut and plentifully filled sandwiches to some excellent daily specials like Steak and Mushroom Pie and Cottage Pie. All home-made naturally. Vegetarians can be catered for. Sunday lunch is traditional and it is as well to book in advance.

USEFUL INFORMATION

OPEN: 11.30-2.30pm. 7-11.00pm
Sun: 12-3.00pm, 7-10.30pm
CHILDREN: Welcome
CREDIT CARDS: Access/Visa/
Diners
LICENSED: Full Licence
GARDEN: Huge Garden & Terrace.

RESTAURANT: Steaks a Speciality
BAR FOOD: Wide choice. Daily
specials
VEGETARIAN: On request
ACCESS FOR THE DISABLED: Yes

THE OAKHILL INN
Inn

Fosse Road,
Oakhill, Bath, Avon
Tel: (0749) 840442

This cheerful, friendly Inn which is near enough 200 years old, sits right in the centre of the village of Oakhill, adjacent to the old church. It is an interesting village with a famous brewery which was reborn not so very long ago and produces extremely good Real Ale, some of which you will find in The Oakhill. The Brewery has become almost a tourist attraction and for that reason a lot of people have discovered that the Inn, which is in no way connected with the brewery, is an excellent place to visit.

It is a typical village pub where the locals congregate and a team spirit prevails. They are enthusiastic dart and pool players and no bad hands at shove ha'penny either. You will find a cross section of people in the three comfortably furnished bars which have a wealth of antique pine panelling. Conversation is lively and you will hear friendly rivalry going on about the various pool or darts matches that have been played against other pubs in the leagues.

A recent additional facility the pub offers is bed and breakfast in attractive and comfortable en-suite bedrooms. An ideal spot to stay if you want to explore Bath and its surrounding areas. The food is good quality home-made pub fare. There is a separate eating space where children are welcome. As well as the varied bar menu there are always daily specials. The mixed grills will satisfy the hungriest of people or if you prefer something less substantial you will not find a better Ploughmans for miles. Sunday Lunch is a traditional roast and it is so popular that booking is advisable.

USEFUL INFORMATION

OPEN: 11-3.00pm 6.30-11.00pm.
Sun: 12-3.00pm. 7-10.30pm
CHILDREN: Welcome
CREDIT CARDS: None taken
LICENSED: Full Licence. Real Ales
GARDEN: Safe garden for children

RESTAURANT: Not applicable
BAR FOOD: Varied menu.
Home-cooked specials
VEGETARIAN: Several dishes
ACCESS FOR THE DISABLED:
Level entrance

THE FROMEWAY
Public House

Frome Road,
Radstock, Nr. Bath, Avon
Tel: (0761) 32116

Here is a Free House which not only serves excellent ale but has a restaurant which is 'Non-smoking' and a butchery next door belonging to the landlords, John and Hilary Denning, so prime quality meat is assured in the bar and the restaurant. The Denning family has been associated with the building since the mid 19th century when it was first built and named 'Huish Road Beer Shop'. Add all these ingredients together and you have the perfect recipe for a fine establishment.

It is a welcoming pub where John and Hilary offer you and your children a real 'home from home'. It has become a regular stop for people travelling the holiday route to the west, as well as for a very lively following who come from near and far to enjoy not only the fun and drink but to sample the excellence of the food prepared by a skilled, imaginative chef. You can stay here too in comfortable en-suite rooms.

Specials on the Blackboard change daily, the sausages and burgers are traditional recipes made on the premises. Vegetarians will love the unusual dishes. Salads are crisp accompanied by Chicken, Roast Beef, Ham or Prawns. Sandwiches, home made soup and Ploughmans are available also. The restaurant specialises in steaks cooked to perfection. Sunday lunch is traditional and very popular. Booking in advance is essential. Good food, good ale, good company and good value sums up The Fromeway.

USEFUL INFORMATION

OPEN: Week: 11-3.00pm, 6-11.00pm
Sun: 12-3.00pm, 7-10.30pm
CHILDREN: Yes
CREDIT CARDS: Visa/Access
LICENSED: Full licence
GARDEN: Yes, Childrens play area. Ample Car Park

RESTAURANT: Home cooking. Prime steaks
BAR FOOD: Daily specials. Wide choice
VEGETARIAN: Yes, several dishes
ACCESS FOR THE DISABLED: Yes

Old Down House,
Tockington, Bristol
Tel: (0454) 413605

THE KITCHEN GARDEN
Restaurant

The B4461 will bring you to The Kitchen Garden Restaurant, Gift Shop and Farm Shop. all three are housed in the converted stables and coach house of Old Down House, an estate that Robert and Alison Bernays have been restoring since 1977. They achieve a bit more every year with Alison being responsible for the restaurant and shops and Robert for the farm and growing things. It is a hive of industry but has that wonderful feeling of peaceful tranquillity which brings people back time and again.

The restaurant gets its name from the large walled garden just outside where the fruit and vegetables are grown. This is where Mary Taylor acquires all the delicious vegetables and fruit that she uses in the dishes on the menu. Everything is freshly prepared in her kitchen – no bought in black forest gateau for her – just the best of local ingredients prepared in a light and attractive way. Although cultivating their own produce generates much more work, it is well worth the labour.

There are simple foods available for example a British 4 Cheese Platter or Jacket Potatoes with home made fillings, and also more exotic fare with daily specials such as Seafood Chowder, Rosemary and Apple Baked Lamb Chops or Braised Beef in Red Wine. For vegetarians there are stuffed Vol-au-Vents or a Kitchen Garden Vegetable Hot Pot. The home made Ice Cream is particularly good. After a meal there are always the gardens to enjoy or further afield the farm and woods to walk in.

USEFUL INFORMATION

OPEN: 9-5.00pm daily except Mondays
CHILDREN: Welcome. High chair provided
CREDIT CARDS: Access/Visa
LICENSED: Selection of Averys wines incl. house wine, local cider & Newquay Steam Beers
GARDEN: Walled with seating. Childrens Play Area

RESTAURANT: The best of English food
BAR FOOD: Not applicable
VEGETARIAN: A main dish each day
ACCESS FOR THE DISABLED: Yes

THE PORTCULLIS INN

Public House/Restaurant

High Street, Todmarton,
Nr Badminton, Avon

Tel: (0454) 21263

For 200 years The Portcullis Inn has been dispensing hospitality to travellers and never better than today in the hands of Seymour Williams and his friendly staff. Todmarton is a conservation area and the pub is totally in keeping with the picturesque village. It is a happy pub with a tremendous atmosphere enhanced in winter by the roaring log fires. The furnishings are comfortable and well lived in. Not only can you eat and drink here but you can also stay in one of the very pretty, en suite bedrooms. The situation makes it an excellent base from which to explore the beauty of Bath, attend the Badminton Horse Trials, walk part of The Cotswold Way which pases by the side of the pub or just wander in the lovely open countryside.

Real Ale enthusiasts will appreciate the range and quality of the beer and the locals will tell you that you will have to go many miles before you can get a better pint.

You can choose to eat in the restaurant which is spacious and comfortable and select from the menu, juicy steaks perfectly grilled or perhaps fresh salmon delicately poached to bring out its flavour. On Sundays there is a traditional roast lunch with a choice of starter, three roast meats, sweet and coffee. All the meals are home cooked and accompanied by fresh vegetables. If you prefer a Bar meal you will find plenty from which to choose. The favourite is the excellent steak and kidney pie. The childrens menu is very popular and there are vegetarian dishes. What is more the price is right!

USEFUL INFORMATION

OPEN: 11-3.00pm, 6-11.00pm.
   Sun: 12-3.00pm, 7-10.30pm
CHILDREN: Welcome. Special menu
CREDIT CARDS: Access/Visa
LICENSED: Full Licence. Small but
   well chosen wine list
GARDEN: Small patio, swings,
   tables & chairs

RESTAURANT: Grills & Poached
   dishes
BAR FOOD: Home cooked. Wide
   choice
VEGETARIAN: 4 dishes daily
ACCESS FOR THE DISABLED:
   Level entrance

41 High Street,
Winterbourne, Avon
Tel: (0454) 773758

THE WHEATSHEAF
Public House/Restaurant

As you come down the High Street you need to exert a little vigilance to spot the entrance to the car park of The Wheatsheaf. Having found it you will drive to the rear and discover one of the pub's charms; its lovely shrub gardens which surround its unique and extensive Pergola. This provides an idyllic setting in which to enjoy ice cool drinks and delicious food in summer time.

Inside, even on the coldest day, Nigel Cairns and his family who have run the pub for ten years, will make you welcome and draw you into the warmth and comfort of their attractive pub. No matter whether you just have a drink in the bar or eat in the restaurant the same friendly atmosphere prevails. The furnishings are just right for the building and on the walls you will find a fascinating collection of old photographs of the area. The Cairns are a dedicated family and their wealth of experience shows in the smooth running of this pleasant pub. It no longer is truly an inn because there is no accommodation.

There is a wide selection of meals here, beautifully prepared and presented. From a choice of several starters there is something for everyone; the home made farmhouse pate is particularly good, followed perhaps by Scotch salmon steak with lobster and dill sauce, Tortellini Carbonara or Beef Stroganoff. Snacks in the bar are super too. Home-made soup of the day with crusty bread is a meal in itself. On Sundays you can choose from the roast meats at the carvery with a selection of fresh vegetables. Included in the price is a choice of starters and several luscious sweets.

USEFUL INFORMATION

OPEN: 11-3.00pm, 6-11.00pm
CHILDREN: If well behaved: welcome
CREDIT CARDS: Amex/Visa/ Access/Diner
LICENSED: Full range wines & beers. Spirits & soft drinks
GARDEN: Seats 60 in Pergola garden

RESTAURANT: Colourful, ample and toothsome
BAR FOOD: Wide choice freshly prepared
VEGETARIAN: 5 dishes
ACCESS FOR THE DISABLED: Level entrance

The glory of the Cloisters at Gloucester Cathedral

INCLUDES:

"Seeing is deceiving.
It's eating that's believing."
James Thurber

*We have King Canute, in 1016, to thank for the glorious 27,000 acres which today make up **The Forest of Dean**. He decreed this should be a royal hunting ground. It is a world of its own with beauty spots, picnic areas, walks, trails, camping sites and a myriad of other activities. It is magical, mysterious, tranquil and yet still it is a source of industry in coal mining and timber. Beneath the tree clad hills, Britain's free miners continue to dig for coal. Quarrying for stone is still active and the last of the stone-cutting factories can be found at **Cannop**.*

*To understand more of the past, a visit to CLEARWELL CAVES near **Coleford** will help and fascinate at the same time. Eight caverns are open to the public in addition to which there are excellent geographical and mining displays which bring home, with clarity, the dangerous and courageous lives our miners have always led. You will be taken on a guided tour into the Bat Chamber, which is the home of hibernating Greater and Lesser Horseshoe Bats in the winter. Since the cessation of mining calcite has grown everywhere and it provides a beautiful backdrop. As you progress through Old Churn, past a miner's coe (rest area) you will reach Chain Ladder Churn, 100ft below the surface, at the deepest point open to the public. It brings home the labour involved in bringing the ore to ground level. I thought about my six year old grandson and realised that boys not much older were expected to manhandle the loads which could well weigh 70lb a time.*

Clearwell Caves are open daily from March 1st – 31st October daily from 10am-5pm

Nearby is a charming place, PUZZLE WOOD, which was created out of some open cast iron workings which were left to gather moss. In the 19th century it was landscaped creating a puzzle path with steps, seats and bridges. You can take picnics here in the very pretty garden. Open daily except Mondays from Easter until October 31st

*Is the Forest more beautifully clad in spring or in autumn? I do not know; either is wonderful. The spring has all the joyous arrival of the soft green unfurling leaves when the ground is carpeted with bluebells, but autumn is a delight to the eye when the Larch turns to russet gold. Wildlife abounds with deer and badgers leading a protected life. Forest sheep thrive and munch their way through the pasture. At NAGSHEAD near **Parkend** you will see birds of all kind in the reserve. Peregrines dominate the scene coming from their breeding ground in **Symonds Yat Rock** in Herefordshire.*

*The Forest is encompassed by three rivers: the mighty Severn, the Wye and the little Leadon. The Severn Valley has everything. It is fertile and full of orchards. Drive along and you will be invited to stop time after time to select fresh fruit, vegetables or flowers from wayside stalls. The Severn Bore is known by most and if you want to see it at its most spectacular then **Newnham** will provide you with a grandstand view. For those who have not met this natural phenomenon before, it is caused by the river flowing seawards and meeting the incoming tide from the Bristol Channel. In the late spring or autumn it reaches its greatest height causing a wave sometimes as high as 10ft. Lesser bores happen throughout the year and give an endless challenge to surfers and canoeists.*

*On the southern edge of the Forest is **Lydney** with THE SWAN HOTEL in which you will be hospitably welcomed and fed on good simple pub fare before setting out perhaps to visit THE DEAN FOREST RAILWAY at the Norchard Steam Centre. The special 'Steam Days' are on Sundays from June to September and every Wednesday afternoon from June until the end of August. If you cannot make one of those days there is still plenty to see with full sized railway engines and coaches plus a museum full of railway related material.*

If you like visiting gardens LYDNEY PARK GARDENS, set in a valley, is full of rhododendrons, azaleas, flowering shrubs, trees, magnolias, and in the spring, daffodils. There is a Roman Temple site and a museum. The park is home to a herd of deer. You are welcome to picnic if you wish. Open Sundays and Wednesdays from the end of April until mid-June from 11-6pm.

*__Cinderford__ and **Coleford** are the two main towns in the Forest, aptly called because of their connection with coal. I found Cinderford interesting more because of its people than its architecture but it does have three excellent hostelries which will fortify you before or after any excursion into the Forest. I have put them in alphabetical order, not preference necessarily. There is THE BRIDGE INN, THE FORGEHAMMER INN and THE GOLDEN LION.*

*Coleford may not be so pretty but it is surrounded by picturesque villages which are a pleasure to explore. Choose either **Newland** or **Broadwell** and you will have chosen well. There is a good pub in each village to add to your enjoyment and you can stay there as well. THE BIRD IN HAND at Broadwell and THE OSTRICH at Newland are both excellent. At **Sling**, which is also a pretty place, you have the advantage of being right on THE OREWAY so perhaps it would not be a bad idea to stay a night or two at the attractive OREPOOL INN which* has a Motel attached. Then at **Staunton** closeby is another good hostelry THE SWAN INN so you really are spoilt for choice.

THE DEAN HERITAGE CENTRE at Camp Mill, **Soudley**, near Cinderford on the B4227, will provide you with a wealth of information and understanding about the Royal Forest. It is a museum of forest life complete with nature trails, craft shops, adventure play areas, barbecue and picnic sites and a very good cafe. It has been superbly converted and todays exhibits explain the industries with the help of a reconstructed mine, a 19th-century coal miner's cottage, a Lightmoor Colliery Engine and a waterwheel.

One constantly changing display is 'The Living Forest' which explores woodland life and history and includes a delightful wildflower garden. A traditional smallholding illustrates the self-sufficient life style of a forester. There is even a Gloucester Old Spot Pig.

For nature lovers who do not want anything too arduous there are three trails. The longest is Foundry Wood Nature Trail which wanders through different woods and can take two hours. Then there is Bradley Hill Woodland Route which is a 2 mile stretch through the oaks and beeches passing old stone quarries and a charcoal burner's camp. One trail that is particularly suited for those in wheelchairs is Soudley Ponds Freshwater Trail which takes about half an hour walking along by the old fish ponds.

If you are more interested in visiting places you may enjoy LITTLEDEAN HALL, which is 2 miles east of Cinderford. This family owned house is renowned for its claims to ghostly hauntings. The site was originally used by the Romans and the remains of a Roman temple were found there in 1984 and identified as Springhead Temple. It is now the largest restored ground plan of such a temple in Britain. Legends abound about Littledean Hall. Most of it seems to stem from 1664 onwards. Tragic events in the dining room led to poltergeists being active. A servant is still said to haunt the landing outside his bedroom. On another occasion two members of the family fell in love with the same woman and ended up shooting each other at the dining table. They have not yet found rest! Phantom bloodstains appear alongside the fireplace, where two officers of the King died in the Civil War. Finally, in amongst this motley collection of ghosts, is a monk who came to give Holy Communion to the family in the days when Catholicism was illegal. No one has slept in the Blue Room with its four poster bed since the 1950s because sleep is disturbed by the sound of footsteps and the clashing of swords! Exciting isn't it? You can visit daily from April to October 10.30am-6pm.

ST BRIAVELS CASTLE southwest of Coleford is also interesting. What is left is the remains of a 12th-century castle adjacent to a Norman church. It stands high above the Wye valley, amid glorious scenery. The church is a beautiful example of Norman and Early English. It is open 10am to dusk daily. There is an interesting custom which happens in the village after evensong on Whit Sunday. Bread and cheese is thrown by a local forester towards the people and it is considered a good omen for the year if you catch a piece. It is a 700 year old custom which used to take place in the church.

Tewkesbury Abbey Church and timber framed houses

It would be a pity not to visit **Newent***, a bustling market town, which has so much that is delightful. THE SHAMBLES was once a slaughterhouse but has been turned into a museum of Victorian life completely furnished in the period. Behind the house is a cobbled square with a blacksmith and carpenters shop. It is open from Easter to October from 10am-6pm except Mondays. It has a licensed restaurant which serves excellent light lunches, teas and coffees.*

If you are interested in Vineyards then two miles north of the village is one that produces a well known English wine THE THREE CHOIRS VINEYARD. It is best to visit between May and October but it is open all the year daily, from 9am-5pm, when you are welcome to tour the vineyard, sample the wine and buy your favourites to enjoy at home.

THE BUTTERFLY CENTRE in Newent is a great attraction. It has a tropical butterfly house, menagerie, aquarium and a natural history exhibition. On the B4216, just outside Newent, is THE FALCONRY CENTRE where eagle and falconry displays are given providing the weather is kind. Open from February to November daily except Tuesdays 10.30-1730.

Who could not love **Tewkesbury**. Situated where the Avon meets the Severn, it is the northern gate to the Cotswolds. It grew up around its Abbey first founded in the 8th century. It is one of England's most magnificent Norman churches and was saved from sacking at the time of the Dissolution when the townspeople decided to buy it. It cost them the vast sum of £453! Everything about is beautiful. Each time I visit I find something new but perhaps the beautiful Quire windows – seven of them, all of which have 14th-century stained glass, and the dazzling splendour of the Beauchamp Chapel, are my favourites. Open in the summer from 7.30am-6pm and in winter until 5pm.

Tewkesbury prospered particularly in the 15th and 16th centuries as you can see from the fine buildings. To see what such a home would look like inside do visit THE LITTLE MUSEUM in Church Street which was built in 1450 and restored in this century. It is simply furnished in solid oak. Open Easter – October Tuesday – Saturday from 10am-5pm.

The broadcaster, journalist and novelist, John Moore was born in Tewkesbury in 1907. His book, Portrait of Elmbury, must have given pleasure to thousands of nature lovers. He could recognise most butterflies, knew the birds and from a young lad he could name the wildflowers. When he died in 1967, the town decided to honour him by restoring the row of medieval cottages in front of the Abbey in Church Street. One of the houses is a museum in which three of the timbered galleries display country items from days gone by, both domestic and agricultural. There is an emphasis on conservation and includes 'Sounds of the Seasons', and 'Where the Severn and Avon meet'. All the displays are based on extracts from John Moore's books. THE JOHN MOORE MUSEUM is open from Easter-October Tuesday to Saturday from 10am-1pm and 2pm-5pm.

Amongst the many good places to eat and drink in Tewkesbury is THE ANCIENT GRUDGE which has a nice tea garden, or CLARETS which specialises in English food plus a very good vegetarian lunch. If you like a Wine Bar then why not try WOODY'S in Barton Street.

Tewkesbury is surround by wonderful villages but who could resist **Bredon** with its picturesque cottages and houses. It is lucky enough to have some good hostelries particularly THE ROYAL OAK.

Cheltenham three hundred years ago was just an ordinary village and not the elegant place we know today. The story of how it became a Spa is undoubtedly far fetched but none the less an enjoyable thought. A resident watched a flock of pigeons who appeared particularly healthy. Daily they came to drink from the same spring. Samples of the water were taken and it was found that it had health giving minerals. This brought people flocking to the town to gain the same benefits as the pigeons and so the town was born. You may not believe it but Cheltonians do – they have seen fit to include a pigeon on the town's crest. By the end of 1783 the first Pump Room was established and it attracted such distinguished visitors as George III and the Duke of Wellington. There is no question that the waters were beneficial and still are.

Pittville Pump Room

Today you can take the waters at the Town Hall as well as the Pittville Pump Room which has to be the most notable of all the Regency buildings. It also houses the PITTVILLE PUMP ROOM MUSEUM OF FASHION on its upper floors where the history of this Regency town is told through two and three dimensional displays of costumes, fashion accessories and jewellery. It is open from April 1st until the end of September, Tuesday-Sunday from 10.30am-5pm, and from October 1st-31st March on Tuesdays-Saturdays from 10.30am-5pm. The whole town has an air of elegance with fine crescents and distinguished mansions. The finest Regency building without doubt is The Promenade, laid out in 1818, it must be one of the most elegant and superior thoroughfares

*in Britain. It was built as a carriage drive leading from the High
Street up to the Spa, now the site of the Queens Hotel. If you want a
good, but simple, hostelry in which to get refreshment after exploring
then do try THE BAYSHILL INN or THE BROWN JUG. Neither
are pretentious and nor will they hurt your pocket. If you like Greek
food and mezze in particular then try THE APHRODITE in Well
Walk. CHRISTOPHERS in Regent Street serves English/Continental
food and in Suffolk Road there is LE CHAMPIGNON SAUVAGE a
reasonably priced classic and modern French restaurant.*

Gloucester Clockmaker's Shop Sign

*Cheltenham is a town of flowers and has many times won awards
in the Britain in Bloom competition. You need go no further than THE
IMPERIAL GARDENS in the heart of the town to enjoy wonderful floral displays. Two museums are worthy of your attention. THE
GUSTAV HOLST BIRTHPLACE MUSEUM is to be found in the
house in which the composer was born. It is furnished in period style and
contains displays of his personal memorabilia. Below stairs is a Victorian
working kitchen with scullery, pantry, laundry and housekeeper's
room. It is open all the year round Tuesdays to Fridays from Noon to
5.30pm and 11am-5.3opm on Saturdays. THE CHELTENHAM ART
GALLERY AND MUSEUM contains a vast range of displays of arts
and crafts as well as an eclectic mix of furniture. There are ceramics,
glass and pewter made between the 17-20th centuries. Oriental ceramics
and armour and 17th-20th century works of art from Britain and*

the Continent, notably Dutch 17th century. Open all the year round Monday-Saturday 10am-5.30pm

Finally, to the county town **Gloucester** *which sits in an envious position and is able to claim it is part of the West country as well as being in the Heart of England. Whichever it wants to be it is bustling and prosperous. A wonderful base from which to explore so many places. Close to the Cotswolds, no distance from the Severn Vale, and a short drive to the Royal Forest of Dean. Wherever you are in the city you cannot miss the Cathedral. It all began in Norman times, a church of strong foundations. It will take you a while to absorb its beauty and magnificence. The 14th-century cloisters and choir were once described to me as symphonies in stone – a perfect description. Roman and medieval Gloucester are closeby, and there are inumerable museums. My favourites are THE GLOUCESTER REGIMENTAL MUSEUM, housed in the historic Custom House in Commercial Road. Open all the year round plus some weekends from 10am-5pm. The other is THE BEATRIX POTTER MUSEUM in College Court. The museum built into the monastery wall features much about the writer's life. Whilst in the little shop, which she chose as a model for her story The Tailor of Gloucester, you can buy all sort of Beatrix Potter bits and pieces including her books. Open all the year round from Monday-Saturday 9.30am-5.30pm*

ROBINSWOOD HILL COUNTRY PARK is the perfect place to enjoy the outdoors, and yet it is only ten minutes from the city. COOPER'S HILL LOCAL NATURE RESERVE lies on a promontory of the Cotswolds overlooking the Severn Vale. These are just one or two of the many places Gloucester has to offer. There are pubs and eating houses everywhere. Two of my favourites are YE OLD FISH SHOPPE, in Hare Lane, in a well preserved timber-framed Tudor building, and a simple pub, THE WHITESMITHS ARMS, where you will always get a friendly welcome.

It is no wonder Charles Dickens described Gloucester as 'A wonderful and misleading city'.

BIRD-IN-HAND INN

Free House

Broadwell,
Nr Coleford, Glos.

Tel: (0594) 32383

Broadwell is 1 mile from Coleford near Mile End Cross Roads situated in the heart of the Forest of Dean. The well known, and very popular, village pub here is the Bird-In-Hand Inn. It is surrounded by wonderful areas in which to walk or visit with Monmouth and its fabulous historic buildings just 6 miles away. The pub is run by two down to earth Lancastrians who came to the Forest of Dean just four years ago.

It has not taken long for Colin and Sue Wheeler to be taken to the heart of the locals and regular visitors. Their philosophy, in keeping with good North Country traditions, is 'Nowt fancy but delicious and plenty of it'. This applies to the food and to the well kept range of beers which includes John Smiths Cask Conditioned Ale. The Bird-in-Hand is only a hundred years old but it lacks nothing in atmosphere and a friendly welcome. It has comfortable bars and a 30 cover restaurant as well as a skittle alley and a nice patio and garden. An ideal place to lunch or dine in at any time of the year.

Food, glorious food, should be the motto of the Bird-in-Hand. It is totally unpretentious but so well cooked and presented that it cannot be faulted. Sue assisted by Angela, daughter of the previous landlord, are the chefs. Their Cauliflower Cheese and Lasagne have gained great acclaim from all over the world. In the Bar you can choose from a variety of home-cooked dishes, opt for steaks, chicken etc or settle for a simple sandwich. In the restaurant, where bookings are necessary, a choice of starters followed by a variety of grills, chicken or fish is the order of the day. Sunday lunch is exceptional and substantial!

USEFUL INFORMATION

OPEN: Food: 12-1.45pm, 7-9.30pm. No meals Monday evening.
CHILDREN: Welcome. Special menu
CREDIT CARDS: None taken
LICENSED: Full Licence
GARDEN: Patio & Garden at rear

RESTAURANT: Traditional English
BAR FOOD: Traditional. Large Choice
VEGETARIAN: Yes. 3 dishes daily
ACCESS FOR THE DISABLED: Yes

85 St Georges Place,
Cheltenham, Gloucestershire
Tel: (0242) 524388

THE BAYSHILL INN
Inn

Surrounded by Regency buildings, right in the heart of Cheltenham, is the Bayshill Inn. Built before 1832 when Cheltenham was just a small village with a High Street, it was originally a coaching inn and has retained many features evident of its previous life. The River Chelt, which you can see at the side of the inn, meandered through fields in those days instead of being surrounded by buildings housing many different sorts of businesses, whose staff are much attached to this friendly establishment. At lunchtime you will find all sorts of people there enjoying the excellent food and soaking up the atmosphere of what is almost still a village pub.

Trevor Wren and his wife have been in the pub for 19 years and have created a very local place with many activities going on. The Bayshill has its own cricket team in the summer and darts, crib and quizzes in the winter which keep the competitive spirit going. It is certainly lively and the staff obviously enjoy their jobs and make sure that everyone is welcome.

Mrs Wren is the cook and she produces good home-made dishes every day. Her braised liver and onions is enormously popular as indeed is the Mexican Pork Spare ribs if you enjoy something spicy. You may be tempted by a Tinkers casserole, mustard chicken breasts, baked ham or a Fishermens pie. If none of these appeal then there is a wide range of standard bar food as well. You will certainly not go hungry nor will you be expected to pay exorbitant prices. It is definitely value for money. There are no Sunday lunches.

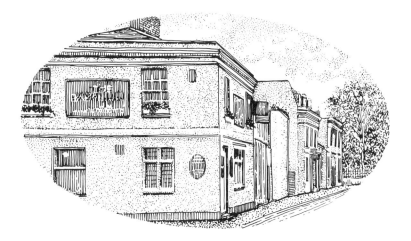

USEFUL INFORMATION

OPEN: Mon-Fri:11-3.00pm,
  5-11.00pm
  Sat:10.30-4.00pm, 6-11.00pm
  Sun:12-3.00pm, 7-10.30pm
CHILDREN: Not allowed
CREDIT CARDS: None taken
LICENSED: Full on Licence
GARDEN: Walled beer garden at rear

RESTAURANT: Not applicable
BAR FOOD: Good home-cooked fare
VEGETARIAN: No
ACCESS FOR THE DISABLED: No

THE BROWN JUG
Public House

242 Bath Road,
Cheltenham, Glos.
Tel: (0242) 521736

If you are fascinated by Toby Jugs you will thoroughly enjoy a visit to The Brown Jug where Derek and Shirley Brimfield, the proprietors, are avid collectors. To date they have 140, mostly rare pieces, including the first ever jug made by Royal Doulton. The Brimfields are a charming and interesting couple who are the second generation to own the pub. You will find the Brown Jug on the south side of Cheltenham, 1½ miles from the town centre, amid the busy Bath road shops and not far from the Gentleman's College where Gloucestershire county hold their annual cricket festival.

It is a sporting pub and has eight teams who use the skittle alley, as well as ladies and gents dart teams plus a crib team. It is lively and friendly, the sort of place in which you are immediately welcome and nobody minds if you would rather have a cup of tea or coffee instead of alchohol.

Food is only available at lunchtimes unless it is for a private function. It is good pub grub with a large choice of dishes all at reasonable prices. The Ploughmans lunch is super and the sandwiches are always made with fresh farmhouse bread and generously filled. The menu includes daily specials and some tasty vegetarian dishes as well. There are no Sunday lunches.

USEFUL INFORMATION

OPEN: 11-2.30pm. 6.30-11.00pm.
   Sun: 12-3.00pm, 7-10.30pm
CHILDREN: No separate room
CREDIT CARDS: None taken
LICENSED: Fully licenced
GARDEN: Rear Yard with flower
   tubs in summer

RESTAURANT: Not applicable
BAR FOOD: Good, wholesome pub
   food
VEGETARIAN: 3 dishes + salads
ACCESS FOR THE DISABLED:
   Welcome but 3 steps

Valley Road,
Cinderford, Gloucestershire
Tel: (0594) 822529

THE BRIDGE INN
Public House

Cinderford is an attractive small town on the outskirts of the Forest of Dean. It is an ideal place to stop for lunch before taking a walk in the forest and what better place to visit for this purpose than The Bridge Inn in Valley Road. This traditional 18th century listed building has always been a pub serving local people and travellers. Today it is very much a hostelry for people who live in the area and who come to visit the pub and the friendly, convivial landlords, Tony and Angie Milliner. Sometimes a local pub can be off putting to visitors who feel that they do not belong but this is definitely not the case here. Everyone is made to feel welcome and part of the warm atmosphere of The Bridge Inn.

The food is good, wholesome down to earth fare which is cooked freshly every day on the premises. If you happen to be partial to Faggots served in a deliciously thick onion gravy then this is definitely the place for you. There are constant menu changes but you will always find something like a first class stew or hot pot which will warm the cockles of the heart on a cold day. The sandwiches are fresh and well filled, the Ploughman's are all served with crispy bread and a garnish and of course there is always a dish for vegetarians by request. The best news is that the prices are very reasonable and the portions plentiful.

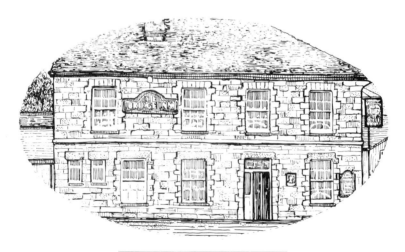

USEFUL INFORMATION

OPEN: Food:10.30-9.00pm,
 Bar:10.30-11.00pm
CHILDREN: Welcome in Lounge
CREDIT CARDS: None taken
LICENSED: Real Ale, Beers: Flowers,
 Marstons, Pencaers, Stella,
 Draught Guiness, Draught
 Ciders
GARDEN: Not applicable

RESTAURANT: Not applicable
BAR FOOD: Good, simple food
VEGETARIAN: Catered for on
 request
ACCESS FOR THE DISABLED:
 Welcome, help available

THE FORGEHAMMER INN
Public House

115 Victoria Street,
Cinderford, Gloucestershire
Tel: (0594) 826662

The name of the inn reflects the origins of Cinderford as an important centre for the Iron Industry starting in the 18th century. This nice, solid building was constructed in 1837 and opened its doors as a pub a year later. It is warm, friendly and comfortable and run by four people, Mr Fairchild and three members of the McKelvie family. It is their aim to make sure you enjoy the food and the fun and go away determined to return as soon as possible.

The Forgehammer is on a southfacing slope on the edge of the town over-looking the Forest so it could not be better sited for those taking a walk before or after lunch. Equally it is ideal for business people who want to escape from their offices at lunchtime or on their way home at night. There was an earlier building on the site, part of which has been incorporated into the pub and with it the ghost of an old sailor who lodged here. Landlords, past and present, regularly hear the sound of skittle balls rolling when the pub is closed.

The fare at The Forgehammer is good, wholesome and inexpensive. In addition to super sandwiches and rolls which are a meal in themselves, there are daily specials, home cooked cottage pie and juicy steak and kidney pies. You can have something as light as an omelette or as tender as an 8oz steak. Chicken, Gammon, Fish, Pork Fillet are all available served either with Jacket Potatoes, Chips or Boiled Potatoes and fresh vegetables or salads. Vegetable pancakes and Lasagne are specially cooked for vegetarians. On Sundays the traditional roast lunch is served between 12-2pm and includes a starter, main course, home-made desserts and coffee.

USEFUL INFORMATION

OPEN: Tues-Thurs: 12-2.30pm.
Fri-Sun: 12-3.00pm Mon-Sat Eve:
7-11.00pm Sun: 7-10.30pm
CHILDREN: Yes. Welcome
CREDIT CARDS: None taken
LICENSED: Full Licence
GARDEN: Yes. Patio

RESTAURANT: Not applicable
BAR FOOD: Wide range. Good
home cooking
VEGETARIAN: 2 dishes always
available
ACCESS FOR THE DISABLED: Yes.

High Street,
Cinderford, Gloucestershire

Tel: (0594) 825146

THE GOLDEN LION
Public House

Cinderford has a very busy and interesting market on Fridays and right in the centre of it is The Golden Lion, a thriving and popular pub which has a lot to offer every day of the week. It has one very important factor, a large car park, the entrance to which is through the archway next to the Butchers. So often pubs in the centre of a town do not have this facility. Pamela and Graham Cooper are the landlords and their friendly, welcoming presence attracts an enthusiastic local following and a number of visitors as well.

Every Saturday and Sunday evening there is a good old fashioned Sing-along. In Summer the Beer Garden is a pleasant place to enjoy a drink or a meal, although it is not suitable for the disabled. There are regular 'Bar-B-Ques' but to ensure you have got the right day it would be as well to ring and confirm. In winter the pub is warm and comfortable. One very useful service offered is a phone in service for lunch so that by the time you arrive your meal will be ready. A great advantage for those in a hurry or who have children with them who hate to be kept waiting. The menu is simple, well cooked and sustaining and everything is reasonably priced. You can enjoy anything from a succulent Sirloin Steak with mushrooms, peas and chips, Chicken roasted or curried, Jumbo Sausage in a hot crusty roll, various filled sandwiches to home-made soup. There are several dishes for Vegetarians including a tasty Broccoli and Cream Cheese pie and for those on a diet, salads are available.

USEFUL INFORMATION

OPEN: Weekdays: 11-4.00pm Sun: 12-3.00pm

CHILDREN: Welcome lounge & dining area

CREDIT CARDS: None taken

LICENSED: Flowers/Whitbread/ Poachers/Stella/Guiness/ Draught Cider

GARDEN: Steps to large lawned area.

RESTAURANT: Meals served in lounge

BAR FOOD: Wide range. Good home cooking

VEGETARIAN: 6-8 dishes available

ACCESS FOR THE DISABLED: No special facilities

THE WHITESMITHS ARMS
Public House

81, Southgate Street,
Gloucester
Tel: (0452) 414770

This has to be one of the most fascinating pubs in Gloucester. It is an old building, one of the oldest near to the docks, with low ceilings and exposed beams, and a very large open log fire which roars away in winter. It may be in the city centre but you feel as though you are visiting a country pub. It is opposite the main entrance to Gloucester's ancient and historic dock and once was a favourite hostelry for sailors, who came ashore from the old sailing ships and were paid off by their masters in the pub itself.

A local artist has painted many of the tall ships, which once were regular visitors to the docks, and they adorn the walls. On the beams you will see some 76 Naval cap tallies – to the uninitiated these are the ribbons bearing the names of the vessels in which the sailors served. Not content with all this, Stuart and Anne Howell, the lively landlords, have a parrot who lives in the bar! It is a great place to visit and is within easy reach of the cathedral and other tourist places.

Food is all home cooked including the pasties. The speciality of the house is a 'Longboat Hot Dog' so called because it contains a home-made sausage 12 inches long. Anne does all the cooking and every day she produces home-made specials as well as normal bar fare. Stuart and Anne run the pub themselves and it was she who started the collection of naval cap tallies because her brother, Gerald, was in the Royal Navy. You will find this a friendly, welcoming pub.

USEFUL INFORMATION

OPEN: 11-2.30pm 6-11.00pm
CHILDREN: Welcome at lunchtimes
CREDIT CARDS: None taken
LICENSED: Full Licence
GARDEN: No

RESTAURANT: Not applicable
BAR FOOD: Wide range
VEGETARIAN: Not specially
ACCESS FOR THE DISABLED:
Level entrance

Hill Street,
Lydney, Gloucestershire
Tel: (0594) 842834

THE SWAN HOTEL

Public House/Hotel/Restaurant

Right in the centre of Lydney and only 5 minutes by car away from the Forest of Dean and its many wonderful walks, is The Swan Hotel. At the rear of the pub there are playing fields, a pretty lake and not so far away The Forest of Dean Steam Railway. So if you decide to come to Lydney and lunch at the Swan you could not be in a better place.

The landlords, Alan and Kate Yeates, and their staff are all local people with a great love of Lydney and the surrounding countryside. They have created a very nice atmosphere and you can be assured of a friendly welcome, fine ale and exceptionally good value pub food. You have the choice of eating in the restaurant or either of the two cosy bars where real coal fires greet you on a cold day. If you want to discover what Lydney looked like in by-gone ears there is a collection of fascinating photographs for you to see. Since those times additions and changes have been made, of course, some for the better such as the Swan's pleasant patio where you can sit on a balmy day. So protected is it that the Yeates manage to grow their own grapes.

The food is imaginative, home cooked and well presented. The two cooks, Elaine and Enza, are gifted. Frequently the Swan has theme weeks when they major on the food and drink of one particular country. Their Italian culinary delights are the most popular, possibly because Enza comes from an Italian family! Bar snacks are filling, home-cooked and the portions generous, whilst in the restaurant the tempting fare makes one's choice even more difficult. Sunday lunch is traditonal and value for money.

USEFUL INFORMATION

OPEN: Food: Mon-Sat:12-2.15pm, 7-9.45pm Sun: 12-2.00pm, 7-9.30pm
CHILDREN: Welcome.
CREDIT CARDS: None taken
LICENSED: Full Licence, plus Coffee
GARDEN: Patio with tables & chairs

RESTAURANT: Good home-cooked fare. Value for money
BAR FOOD: Extensive range. Meals & snacks.
VEGETARIAN: Always 6 dishes plus sandwiches
ACCESS FOR THE DISABLED: Level entrance

THE OSTRICH
Public House & Accommodation

Newland, Nr Coleford,
Gloucestershire
Tel: (0594) 33260

Newland is one of those pretty picturesque villages that nestles into the rolling wooded hills alongside the scenic Wye Valley. Nothing hurries the life style of this delightful place and within it is The Ostrich Inn which dates back to the early 13th century. At that time it was a hospice for workers building 'The Cathedral of the Forest'. It is one of those pubs that just welcomes you in and from the moment you step through the low doorway you know it is going to be a happy visit.

Richard and Veronica Dewe are the landlords and from the day that they took over in the autumn of 1990, they have worked unceasingly to make it the sort of pub that they themselves would enjoy. There are no juke boxes, no one armed bandits and the superior quality food and drink are at very affordable prices. To this cosy environment people come time and again. You have only to see the busy bar to recognise that the Dewe's simple formula is highly successful.

The menu varies with the season making full use of fresh vegetables and herbs, many of which are grown locally. The choice of about ten main dishes invariably includes such local specialities as Venison Pie and Game Casserole. There are starters and tasters, Honeyed chicken in a mild curry sauce, Duck pancakes, super puddings and Vegetarian dishes but never chips! There is a wide choice of Bar snacks, in fact something to suit everyone.

USEFUL INFORMATION

OPEN: Mon-Sat: 11.30-3.00pm, 6-11.00pm Sun: 12-3.00pm, 7-10.30pm
CHILDREN: In restaurant & garden
CREDIT CARDS: None taken
LICENSED: Fully licenced
GARDEN: Attractive walled garden, tables & chairs

RESTAURANT: Good quality & affordable
BAR FOOD: Wide range. Cold food available
VEGETARIAN: Yes. Two-Three dishes
ACCESS FOR DISABLED: None

St Briavels Road,
Sling, Nr. Coleford,
Royal Forest of Dean

Tel: (0594) 33277

THE OREPOOL INN
Inn & Motel

The Royal Forest of Dean is recognised as an area of outstanding natural beauty with breathtaking scenery and woodland walks within a few miles. Situated on the 'Oreway', a medieval route carrying iron ore from the surrounding district, is The Orepool Inn and Motel. It is a fascinating place built in the mid 17th century for the purpose of providing an ale house for the miners who extracted the ore from the adjacent drift mine.

Jim and Joan Wilson, the proprietors, have done much to preserve the old part of the inn whilst ensuring that the new motel extension has every modern convenience that a guest might require. It is a wonderful spot in which to stay for the sheer pleasure of the stunningly beautiful area and to indulge oneself in the hospitality, the food, the extensive range of wines, beers, spirits and Real Ale.

In addition, there is a Pool and Games Room and a Skittle Alley. At Sunday lunchtime in the summer months you will find a brass band playing in the large garden, weather permitting, where you can both eat and drink. In the restaurant and the bar there is an extensive choice of dishes; something to suit everyone. On Sundays a traditional lunch is served which is very popular and it is advisable to book.

USEFUL INFORMATION

OPEN: Mon-Sat: 11.00am-11.00pm.
Sun: 12-3.00pm, 7-10.00pm
CHILDREN: Welcome
CREDIT CARDS: Visa/Access/
Amex/Mastercard
LICENSED: Full Licence
GARDEN: Large Garden. Childrens
play area. Brass Band plays
Summer Sunday lunch

RESTAURANT: Traditional food
BAR FOOD: Wide choice, home
cooked dishes
VEGETARIAN: 2-3 dishes daily
ACCESS FOR THE DISABLED: Full
facilities

THE SWAN INN
Public House

Ledbury Road,
Staunton, Gloucestershire
Tel: (0452) 840323

This nice pub situated on the A417 Gloucester to Ledbury Road at Staunton Cross roads, has been giving sustenance to weary travellers since 1750. Staunton is a pleasant village surrounded by farmland, and is very much a community with the church and the Swan being the focal points. You will always find local people at the bar and they, together with the friendly landlords, Graham and Judy Jones make sure that visitors feel welcome.

The Swan was once a coaching inn and its three feet thick walls plus the roaring log fires make sure you feel the warmth in winter as you step through the door into the comfortable bar. In the summer the Garden Patio has a Barbecue area which is a very pleasant way of spending time. It is definitely a pub for all ages; young farmers play skittles, the senior citizens mull over the past whilst supping their ale and in the super conservatory style restaurant which is a recent addition, people dine in delightful surroundings.

The emphasis is on hospitality and good food in a country pub and this has been achieved. The restaurant has a full a la carte menu which will suit all tastes and the bar menu, apart from the usual things one would expect to find, has super daily specials which include dishes prepared with local game and Elvers, served in a traditional style, when in season. On Sundays a three course roast lunch is served between 12-2pm supported by salads and sandwiches in the bar. If you are there when a Barbecue is in progress try the Carribbean Spicy Kebabs!

USEFUL INFORMATION

OPEN: Mon-Fri: 11-3.00pm,
6.30-11.00pm Sat: 11-11.00pm
Sun: 12-3.00pm, 7-10.30pm
CHILDREN: Welcome. Garden &
swings
CREDIT CARDS: Access/Visa
LICENSED: Full with supper
extension
GARDEN: Garden Patio with
Barbecue

RESTAURANT: Full A La Carte
Menu
BAR FOOD: Wide Selection Bar
Meals & Snacks
VEGETARIAN: 5 always + specials
at random
ACCESS FOR THE DISABLED:
Access to wheelchairs

Main Road, Bredon,
Tewkesbury, Gloucestershire
Tel: (0684) 72393

THE ROYAL OAK
Public House

Bredon is one of the prettiest and most picturesque villages in an area full of beautiful places to visit. The Royal Oak, where mine hosts are Ian and Dee Collinson, is one of the focal points of the village. It is the epitome of a friendly, warm and comfortable country pub where people love to gather for a drink, some lively chatter and maybe a game of darts. It has a flourishing local trade which always is a sign of a well run public house where the beer is well kept. There is plenty of parking space and it is an ideal spot to rest a while before taking a walk or perhaps driving into nearby Tewkesbury to look at the glorious abbey.

When you eat at The Royal Oak you can be assured that the food is always fresh and home cooked in the very best traditional manner. There are some popular simple dishes such as home cured ham, egg and chips or Steak and Kidney Pie or perhaps Rainbow Trout or a Fillet steak might be more to your liking. Basket Meals are available and so are deliciously filled Jacket Potatoes served with a side salad. If you have a sweet tooth then the Chocolate Fudge cake or Profiteroles and Chocolate Sauce will tempt you. There are always dishes for vegetarians one of which is a particularly good Cauliflower and Potato Bake. On Sundays you will find a traditional three course lunch with succulent meats, crisp roast potatoes and fresh vegetables. It really is excellent value for money.

USEFUL INFORMATION

OPEN: 12-3.00pm, 6.30-11.00pm
Food:12-2.00pm daily. 7-10.00pm
weekdays. Sun: 7-9.00pm
CHILDREN: Allowed when eating
CREDIT CARDS: None taken
LICENSED: Full Licence. Well kept
beer
GARDEN: Courtyard. Garden
summer 1991

BAR FOOD: Traditional home cooked
RESTAURANT: Not applicable
VEGETARIAN: Yes. 3-4 dishes
ACCESS FOR DISABLED: No

The house of clothier, Daniel Packer, Painswick

INCLUDES:

"Go thy way, eat thy bread with joy,
and drink thy wine with a merry heart: . . ."
Ecclesiastes

THE COTSWOLDS

A birds eye view of the Cotswolds is all that I am able to give you in the permitted space. At worst it will whet your appetite to know more and at best it will instil in you a little of the sheer joy the area has given me over many years.

For the ardent walker there is almost one hundred miles of footpath which will take you through ever changing scenery, sometimes climbing steeply or descending abruptly, following the escarpment for much of the time. It will never fail to delight you as you walk along beside burbling streams, over rickety bridges, through woods and in and out of 'kissing gates'. You will sometimes find yourself on a golf course and the next moment wandering through fields of corn. There are long barrows and hill forts and picturesque Cotswold villages. The route will take you from Kelston Round Hill near Bath through Tormarton and the Sodburys, Nibley Knoll and Stinchcombe Hill, Freocester Beacon, Painswick Hill Fort, Cooper's Hill and Birdlip, by the Devil's Chimney high up on Leckhampton to the highest point in the Cotswolds at Cleeve Cloud and then down to Winchcombe, the ancient capital of Mercia. Not far on is Hailes and then another climb to Beckbury Camp. Down again to Stanway and Stanton on to Broadway and so to Chipping Camden. Much too long a trail for most of us but you can join it anywhere along the way.

*I am going to start my journey more sedately by visiting **Bishops Cleeve** just two miles outside Cheltenham where, near the racecourse, there is a charming thatched pub THE KING'S HEAD, which I always enjoy. Both **Prestbury** and Bishops Cleeve tend to get forgotten or be considered part of Cheltenham, yet they are charming villages in their own right. **Winchcombe** next which wreaks of history. The town grew round its abbey in the 8th century but almost nothing remains, except for part of the gallery which you can see in THE GEORGE INN, another fine establishment. By the 16th century, Winchcombe was revelling in the wealth brought by the tobacco industry. Fine houses were built and the character of the town was born. If you go into the FOLK MUSEUM at the Town Hall you can discover all about it. It is open from April 1st – 31st October, Monday to Saturday 10am-5pm. Winchcombe also has Britain's oldest private railway museum. It is a fascinating collection of railway memorabilia including one of the country's largest collections of cast iron and lineside notices. WINCHCOMBE RAILWAY MUSEUM is open daily from 1pm-6pm.*

It would be sacrilegious to miss a visit to SUDELEY CASTLE which is close to Winchcombe, just off the A46. It is rich in history and contains some fine art treasures. The grounds are beautiful and include an Elizabethan garden, and there are regular falconry displays. You will need to allow some considerable time here if you are to get the most out of it. It is open daily from April 1st to October 31st. The grounds and craft workshops from 11-5.30pm and the castle from 12-5pm.

HAILES ABBEY is a beautiful medieval abbey lying in ruins but with a romanticism about it that makes it a must for visitors. Open 15th March-15th October, Monday to Saturday from 9.30am-6.30pm and on Sundays from 2pm-6.30. From mid October to mid March it is open Monday-Saturday from 9.30-4pm and Sundays from 2pm-4pm. Then there is STANWAY HOUSE, a golden Jacobean manor, just to the north east of Hailes, which demands your attention. The house has only changed hands once in the last 1300 years or thereabouts. It is full of beautiful things and outside, the gardens are a joy. Open June 1st-August 31st, Tuesdays and Thursdays only from 2pm-5pm. You can get a very good tea here in the old bakehouse.

Snowshill

And so to **Snowshill** just west of the tiny hill-top village of **Bourton-on-the-Hill** with its church that has a fine Norman south arcade. SNOWSHILL MANOR is a charming Tudor house with a 17th-century facade. It has an incredible mixture of displays inside. Anything from weavers and spinners tools to Japanese armour and musical instruments. The owner filled the house so full that he had to move to an adjoining cottage in the courtyard to give his collection more space. His name was Charles Wade and his coat of arms bears the motto 'Nequid Pereat' – 'Let Nothing Perish'. There is no question that he stuck to this. The terraced gardens with an abundance of old roses are a delight to the eye and the nostril. The Manor is open from April to October at weekends from 11-1pm and 2-6pm, and also from May to the end of September from Wednesday to Sunday from 11am-1pm and 2pm-4pm.

South of Bourton-on-the-Hill is SEZINCOTE, famous for its house and garden. The house was remodelled by a wealthy 18th-century Nabob, Sir Charles Cockerell. He loved all things oriental and had his house constructed in Indian style with oriental gardens. So impressed was the Prince Regent when he came to visit in 1807 that he decided to use a similar design for his own Brighton Pavilion.

Broadway by rights should not appear in this book for it is in Worcestershire but who can resist it. Unfortunately for those who love it, the village has become too popular. It is so attractive that it brings people from all over the world to savour its loveliness only to find that the overcrowding disguises its true beauty. See it early in the morning or just as the evening is drawing in and you will see the true Broadway. There can be very few people who have not heard of THE LYGON ARMS one of the country's leading inns. A place of charm, character and furnished quite beautifully with genuine country furniture. It goes without saying that the food and the hospitality are superb. Stay there and you will be cocooned in comfort.

One of the great Cotswold wool towns in the Middle Ages was **Chipping Camden**. It is still an attractive market town and well worth a visit particularly if you want to see a flawless example of a 'wool' church. It represents the wealth of the time, and piety thrown in for good measure. It has a splendidly decorated West tower, tall nave arcades with light that floods from the clerestory and window over the chancel arch. The church is open from 8am until dusk. THE WOOLSTAPLERS HALL, which was a 14th-century merchant's house, now holds a wonderful collection of things pertinent to the history of the town. It is open from October 31st – March, from Tuesday to Saturday 10am-5pm and Sundays from 2-pm-5.30pm. April 1st until the end of September daily from 10am-5.30pm and Sundays from 2pm-5.30pm.

Gardens always attract me and right in the High Street is the ERNEST WILSON MEMORIAL GARDEN which opens daily. It is in memory of Ernest Wilson who was dedicated to the study of Chinese and Japanese botanical specimens. Two other gardens are quite near the town. HIDCOTE MANOR GARDENS lying 3 miles to the northeast, was *created early this century by a noted horticulturist, Major Lawrence Johnstone. He strove successfully to build a series of small formal gardens separated by walls or hedges of different species. If you are there in July you may be lucky enough to catch a performance of a Shakespeare play which takes place in the grounds. If you would like details telephone (0684) 850051. The gardens are open daily from April until October, except for Tuesdays and Fridays, 11am-8pm.*

The House of William Greuel, Chipping Camden

KIFTSGATE COURT is right by Hidcote and is full of unusual plants and shrubs as well as a wonderful display of hydrangeas. Open Sunday, Wednesday, Thursday from April 1st until September 30th from 2pm-6pm.

Back in Chipping Camden, THE COTSWOLD HOUSE HOTEL is not only an excellent place to stay but it also has an all day eaterie. If you want a good pub I can recommend THE VOLUNTEER INN in St Catherine's Square.

Blockley *comes under the heading too of villages you should not miss. It is probably the most unspoilt of all the Cotswold villages. It suffered, like so many others, from the decline of the woollen industry but it was saved by the continued production from its eight silk mills. Many of the houses on Blockley Brook at the southern end of the village were once mills. It has a collection of genuinely ancient inns which will* *provide you with food and particularly good Real Ale. It is the sort of place that will have your cameras hard at work.*

*Another small town with much character is **Moreton-in-Marsh**. It is right on the Fosseway and has a High Street full of splendid 18th and 19th-century buildings. Just outside the town in **Upper Oddington** is a 16th-century pub of Cotswold stone, THE HORSE AND GROOM, an ideal place to stay, drink or eat. From there you could sally forth to visit BATSFORD ARBORETUM just 1 miles west of Moreton. It has the largest private collection of rare trees in the country, planted in the 1880s by Lord Redesdale when he returned to Britain from his embassy posting in Tokyo. The views are stunning and the magnolias and maples stand out in my mind as being especially wonderful. Spring and autumn are probably the best times of the year to visit because of the astounding beauty of the colour. Open April 1st – October 31st from 10am-5pm.*

*High on a hill beside the Roman Fosse Way is **Stow-in-the-Wold**. It was a centre for wool in medieval times and today is a picturesque town which will give you a great deal of pleasure and in which you can visit some excellent hostelries. THE KINGS ARMS in Market Square is an old Posting House where once King Charles I rested his weary head, and then there is THE QUEENS HEAD which Sporting Life described as 'the best pub in the Cotswolds'. Stow is renowned for its antique shops, of which there are many, in and around the market square.*

*Another village just off the Fosse Way is the incomparable **Bourton-on-the-Water**. It is infinitely photographable and because of this, like Broadway, it does suffer from a surfeit of visitors. There are several places to visit, amongst them THE MODEL RAILWAY EXHIBITION which will endear itself to young and old with its 400sq ft of model railway layouts. It is open daily from 11am-5.30pm from April to September and at weekends from October-March. At the New Inn in the High Street is THE MODEL VILLAGE which has been in situ for 50 years and is a model of the village built in Cotswold stone. It is open daily throughout the year from 9am-dusk. In 3 ¹/₂ acres of enclosed parkland behind Rissington Road is THE BIRDLAND ZOO GARDEN, with a penguin rockery, tropical bird house and some fine floral displays. It is open daily from 10am-6pm, April to October and from 10-4pm November to March. If you enjoy cars and cycles from past years you will enjoy THE COTSWOLDS MOTOR MUSEUM which is housed in an 18th-century watermill. What I enjoyed most though was the extraordinary collection of old advertising signs which made me quite nostalgic for my childhood days. Open February – November daily from 10am-6pm. I can recommend both THE MOUSE TRAP INN and*

THE OLDE CHARM in Bourton when you are in need of refreshing the inner man.

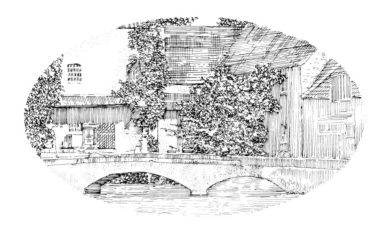

Bourton-on-the-Water

Two more places beginning with the letter B are favourites of mine in the Cotswolds. **Burford**, which is actually in Oxfordshire. I have many happy memories of this delightful village with its steep main street leading down to the river Windrush from the Wolds. There is only one way to see Burford and that is on foot. South of Burford is THE COTSWOLD WILDLIFE PARK with its expansive enclosures, reptile house and wonderful landscaped gardens.

Bibury, in the 17th century, was a famous horse racing centre and home of England's oldest racing club. Take a look at Arlington Row with its picturesque Cotswold Cottages. ARLINGTON MILL MUSEUM is built on a Domesday site. It is a 17th-century corn mill, which, with the adjoining cottages, has become a museum with 17 exhibit rooms. It opens its doors from mid March to mid November daily from 10.30-7pm but only at weekends in the winter.

Northleach is very special because of its church mainly which dominates the small town. It is magnificent, built in the 15th century when the woollen industry was at its height. The south porch has original statues under canopied niches, great crocketed pinnacles and a stair turret crowned with a delightful spirelet. Look inside the ornate vaulted

163

porch at the corbel and suddenly you are brought back to every day things; it is a cat fiddling to three mice. The pulpit is goblet shaped and the 14th-century font is decorated with carved heads and angels playing medieval instruments. It is open daily from 9am-dusk. Two other wool churches almost match it, the one in Chipping Camden and the other at Cirencester.

*A short journey along the A436 will bring you to **Andoversford**, not really comparable with the places we have been talking about but I did happen across a friendly pub here, THE ROYAL OAK INN which is worth making a detour.*

*On a steep sided tributary of the Coln is **Chedworth** which sits on either side of a steep valley making the cottages look as though they are growing out of it. Indeed, I was told that they have more rows of windows that open away from the hill than open on to it. Its pub THE SEVEN TUNS is a good place in which to get sustenance before tackling a visit to CHEDWORTH ROMAN VILLA. There are several paths and bridleways from the village which lead into woods and on to the Villa. The Roman Villa is quite often regarded as the finest in Britain. You realise when you see its size, some 32 rooms and separate bathrooms, just how sophisticated the Romans were.*

*To the south of the A40 from Northleach to Burford, the Cotswolds are split by fertile river valleys along which villages have grown. The wolds of this southern section are not as well populated as the north. The difference between the populated valley and empty wold is marked. The first valley was cut by the river Leach that flows by Northleach, and in its upper reaches the leach drains bleak wold. It is not as pretty as the Coln nor does it have the character of the Windrush, but it is beautiful and gives its name to **Lechlade**, the town that separates the Cotswolds from the Thames valley. It is a nice small town well known to Thames cruisers for it is the highest point of navigation on the river. There are some fine Georgian buildings and a church whose roof boss above the nave shows two carved wrestlers. It is similar to Lincoln Cathedral but nowhere near as grand. THE TROUT INN is the place to eat.*

*It would be worth stopping at **Fairford** on your way from here to **Cirencester**, mainly to see the splendid Perpendicular church built at the end of the 15th century by John Tame, a wool stapler and cloth merchant. Its greatest glory is the 28 windows of wonderful coloured glass, contemporary with the church. Who could find a better place to stay or eat than at the 15th-century coaching inn, THE BULL HOTEL.*

I am never quite sure what I expect to find in Cirencester but I know I love the graceful Georgian buildings in which this interesting town is rich. The church is dazzling and will give you hours of pleasure just wandering around and everlastingly finding something new on which to comment. It is open in summer from 9.30am – 6.30pm and in winter until 5pm. You must visit THE CORINIUM MUSEUM in Park Street which contains one of the largest collections of Roman artefacts in the country. There are full scale reconstructions of the Roman way of life as it was in this town. There is not only a full size triclinium (dining room) and kitchen but also superb mosaic floors. To complete it there is a Roman garden. Skilfully, the Museum has made sure that although the Roman theme predominates there is still plenty of room for an excellent chronological sequence of Cotswold history on display. Open 31st March to 1st October Tuesday to Saturday from 10am-5pm and on Sundays from 2pm-5pm. From April 1st until September 30th it is open daily from 10am-5.30pm and from 2pm-5.30pm on Sundays.

A view of distant Fairford

If you would rather be out of doors, at the top of Cecily Hill is the entrance to CIRENCESTER PARK, a wonderful expanse of greenery which is owned by Earl Bathurst. Cars and cycles are not permitted, but you can walk or ride to your hearts content, in woodland and parkland laid out in the 18th century by the 1st Earl Bathurst helped by his friend, the poet, Alexander Pope.

I found a good, homely pub here, THE DRILLMANS ARMS, but if you would prefer something different then THE COUNTRY STYLE

COFFEE HOUSE or THE MAD HATTER are both good eateries which will not break the bank. If you like wholefood then try THE BREWERY COFFEE HOUSE, Cirencester Workshops, which is a licensed coffee house for daytime eating. It has the most scrumptious home-made cakes. Two places to stay, one of which is part of Forte hotels, are THE FLEECE HOTEL which is an old Tudor coaching inn, and the other is THE KING'S HEAD HOTEL in Market Place, also an historic coaching inn almost opposite The Fleece. In either you will be treated with courtesy and old fashioned hospitality.

There is another delightful pub in the village of **Oakridge Lynch** which you will find on the Cirencester to Stroud road. THE BUTCHERS ARMS is everything a village pub ought to be. You could call here perhaps after a visit to **Sapperton**, a pretty village away from the main roads at the western edge of Cirencester Park. At one time it was remarkable for the Thames and Severn Canal which went through a mile long tunnel under the Cotswolds on its descent to Stroud. That has gone and the tunnel is not accessible although the entrance has been restored. What it does have though is a good canal pub at either end THE DANEWAY ARMS and THE TUNNEL.

South of Cirencester is **Tetbury**, one of the most popular of Cotswold villages. It is comparatively unspoilt and has a fine parish church which is a good example of Gothic restoration. The Market house too has been well restored. The village has come into prominence since this part of Gloucestershire became the home of members of the Royal Family. There is a pub just two miles away on the Cirencester Road called THE TROUBLE HOUSE INN which is very special. It earned its name but today is a peaceful, welcoming establishment where the landlords will only be too happy to explain why it is so called!

WESTONBIRT HOUSE and GARDEN, roughly three miles south of Tetbury, is an excellent place to visit. The Arboretum contains one of the world' finest collection of temperate trees and shrubs. It is a place of startling contrasts. In the spring the magnificent rhododendrons bloom and in autumn the fantastic colour of the leaves are stunning. The house is only open twice a year to the public but the Arboretum is open daily all the year round from 10am-8pm.

I have visited CHAVENAGE HOUSE twice and enjoyed it each time. It is on the B4014 just northwest of Tetbury. It is an Elizabethan manor house thought to be haunted by Charles I and has Cromwellian associations. It has a great air about it which is intangible but charming. Open from May to September on Thursdays and Sundays from 2pm-5pm.

I will mention **Stroud** and **Nailsworth** because they are in the area I am writing about but neither appeals to me, although, if you search, you will find architectural gems in both places. I would rather spend time in two other delightful villages. The first is **Nympsfield** which was once a coaching stop bustling with carriages and hostelries. Today there is only one coaching inn left but it keeps a high standard and that is THE ROSE AND CROWN. If you climb the hill out of Nympsfield to the picnic area of COALEY PEAK you will be rewarded by some of the best views in the Cotswolds.

At **Painswick,** which is more of a small town than a village, built on a hillside, you will find somewhere that will provide you with all the photographs you could possibly require to remind you of a visit to the Cotswolds. It has flower decked stone cottages lining the steep, narrow, cobbled streets. The medieval church of St Mary the Virgin is beautifully restored and it is famous for its superlative collection of 17th and 18th-century table tombs, many of them erected for the rich clothiers whose money made it such a fine place. You will find inside the church a leaflet which will guide you on a fascinating 'tomb trail' amongst the 99 luxuriant yews planted in 1792. Only 99 because the devil threatened to destroy them all and the village as well if ever there were 100! Open to visitors from 9am until dusk. What finer way to end a visit here than to go to THE COUNTRY ELEPHANT, which incidentally has the most delightful garden, and where you will be welcomed and revived with first class food, drink and hospitality typical of the Cotswolds.

THE ROYAL OAK
Public House

Gloucester Road, Andoversford,
Cheltenham, Gloucestershire

Tel: (0242) 820335

Andoversford is only 5 miles from Cheltenham. Just 50 yards from the main A40 turn off you come into the village and almost immediately see The Royal Oak which has stood there for nearly 400 years. It has not always been a pub and was built originally as a farmhouse becoming a coaching house sometime in the 19th century. Apart from Andoversford being a pleasant village it also has a busy cattle market once a week, and annually is the host in May for horse sales as part of Stow Fair week. Just a short drive from the pub you will find Kilkenny viewpoint which on a fine and clear day gives you the most superb outlook over the Cotswolds.

The Royal Oak is very much a village pub and most of the staff were born and bred in the area. Sharon and Ian Macdonald, the landlords, themselves have a lot of local knowledge and they and their staff are all prepared to share it with you. Interestingly one of the lady members of staff is one of the only women in the Cotswolds to have kept up the traditional dry stone walling process and has found herself featured in several Sunday colour supplements and other interviews. If you have ever watched dry stone walling being carried out you will know what a skilled business it is. You can eat the excellent food either in the bar or in an upstairs restaurant. It is good home cooked fare with a menu that changes with the seasons. At lunchtime or in the evening you can choose from the full a la carte menu or have something simpler such as a well filled sandwich made with fresh granary bread. There are salads of all kinds, indeed something to satisfy any palate.

USEFUL INFORMATION

OPEN: 11-2.30pm, 6-11.00pm Sun:
  12-3.00pm, 7-10.30pm
CHILDREN: Welcome
CREDIT CARDS: None taken
LICENSED: Full licence
GARDEN: Large sunny patio with
  tables

RESTAURANT: A la carte
BAR FOOD: Good home-cooked fare
VEGETARIAN: Several dishes
ACCESS FOR THE DISABLED: Yes
  except res't.

Church Road, Bishops Cleeve,
Cheltenham, Gloucestershire
Tel: (0242) 673260

THE KINGS HEAD

Inn

The Kings Head, just three miles from Cheltenham, on the A435 Evesham road, is one of those wonderful old 16th century black and white inns that one always hopes to find but seldom does. For generations it has been a favourite watering hole for people attending the races at the Cheltenham course about two miles away. It is a listed building standing next to an old tythe barn and is believed to be the oldest inhabited building in the village.

No one could ask for a better atmosphere. It is everything you would expect to find in a traditional English pub. The timber beams are genuine, the flagstone floor bears the marks of footprints of hundreds of years. In winter a log fire roars away in the vast hearth and there is an air of total contentment about the place. There is no doubt that Peter and Mary Millar who are the proprietors, have much to do with the cheery welcome you get from them and their staff.

Peter has earned himself a well deserved reputation for the cask conditioned ale that he serves. From the kitchen comes the tempting smell of the 'Daily Specials' to which regulars look forward. In addition to these, there is a range of bar food including a super Ploughmans lunch served with crisp bread. Sunday lunch is not available at present and food is served only at lunchtime. This is a pub to remember with affection and a resolve to return again as soon as possible.

USEFUL INFORMATION

OPEN: 11-2.30pm, 6-11.00pm
CHILDREN: Not in bar area
CREDIT CARDS: None taken
LICENSED: Full licence
GARDEN: Beer garden

RESTAURANT: Not applicable
BAR FOOD: Daily specials & pub grub
VEGETARIAN: 2 dishes daily
ACCESS FOR THE DISABLED: Level entrance

THE MOUSETRAP INN

Inn

Lansdowne,
Bourton-on-the-Water,
Gloucestershire

Tel: (0451) 20579

Bourton-on-the-Water is one of the most popular and most delightful villages in the Cotswolds. Its only drawback is the difficulty one has in parking, but a visit to The Mousetrap Inn, just 250 yards from the centre, takes care of that: it has a large car park. That is not its only virtue. Bernard and Jenny Harris, the proprietors, have made certain of that. The welcome you get is a warm one in true Cotswold style and they have developed this 17th-century inn in the nicest way. Not only can you eat here but you can stay for bed and breakfast as well. It is ideally situated to allow you to explore the Cotswolds and visit some of the many attractions such as Birdland, The Model Village, the Motor Museum, and the Perfumerie.

Food and drink are important naturally and you will find that Bernard knows how to care for the excellent range of Beers and Ciders he serves, whilst Jenny produces a super selection of reasonably priced and mostly home-cooked dishes. The pub is noted for its 'Desperate Dans Cow Pie' and also for a very tasty Rabbit pie, something rarely seen. In addition there are many other dishes from which to choose including fish, poultry and a very good Cottage Pie. For the exceptionally hungry there are large sirloin steaks cooked whichever way you care to choose. Whatever is your preference you will not go hungry. Whilst you wait for your meal take a look at all the memorabilia from the famous 'Mousetrap' play.

USEFUL INFORMATION

OPEN: 12-3.00pm, 6.30-11.00pm
CHILDREN: Permitted
CREDIT CARDS: None taken
LICENSED: Full licence
GARDEN: Tables at front of pub

RESTAURANT: Dining room with good range
BAR FOOD: Mostly home-cooked with specialities
VEGETARIAN: 2/3 dishes daily
ACCESS FOR THE DISABLED: Level entrance

1, The Chestnuts,
Bourton-on-the-Water,
Gloucestershire

Tel: (0451) 20244

THE OLDE CHARM

Restaurant, Bed & Breakfast

The Olde Charm is in the middle of Bourton--on-the-Water, one of the most picturesque villages in the Cotswolds. The land outside this delightful establishment is called 'The Chestnuts' because of the three large chestnut trees which form two, almost perfect, arches. It faces the river, and overlooks the square giving a charming view from each of the Olde Charm's rooms. A fitting site for a venue which offers excellent fare and a gracious and impressive standard of accommodation.

Helen and Tony Goss are the proprietors who, with wisdom and care, have maintained the 300 years old building keeping and enhancing many of its original features. The hallway and rooms have exposed beams and the floors slope every which way. The restaurant is large and elegant in its burgundy decor with dark Jacobean oak tables and chairs, and brass ceiling fans making it light and airy particularly in the summer months. The service is unobtrusive and very professional. The Goss's are particularly fortunate in their staff; the latter are all, incidently, members of one family.

Food is available all day, the hours depending upon the time of year. Lunch offers excellent home-made soups, fresh salads, succulent roast meats, and a selection of desserts, gateaux and ice creams. Grills are available in the afternoon as well as their 'Cotswold cream tea' which is very popular. The menu changes in the evening and there is a licensed bar. The accommodation rooms are beautifully appointed and absolutely spotless, all with en suite facilities.

USEFUL INFORMATION

OPEN: Approx 10.30-9.30pm
CHILDREN: Yes, no under 5 facilities
CREDIT CARDS: Access/Visa/
Amex/Diners
LICENSED: Beer, lager, spirits, wines
GARDEN: No

RESTAURANT: Trad. Eng: Roasts,
Grills, Salads
BAR FOOD: Not applicable
VEGETARIAN: No.
ACCESS FOR THE DISABLED:
Level entrance/toilets

THE SEVEN TUNS

Public House

Queen Street,
Chedworth, Gloucestershire
Tel: (0285) 720242

In the midst of the very picturesque and traditional village of Chedworth near the head of the Chedworth valley, stands a typical stonebuilt, 17th-century Cotswold pub. It is a small, comfortable and very friendly establishment run by Brian and Barbara Eacott. They are just the right people for the Seven Tuns. They have a nice sense of fun, are very popular with the locals knowing just how to look after visitors who find their way to this truly rural area.

The Seven Tuns served the community from the mid-17th century until 1948 as an ale and cider house. At that time it was granted a wine and spirits licence. The name refers to the seven chimneys the pub once had. Inside there are two bars, a games room and a skittle alley. The small lounge bar only seats 16-18 people so it is advisable to come early especially on Sundays. Outside there is a charming walled garden which was once the village Pound, through which runs a small stream, an ideal setting for balmy summer's days. The food is excellent. At lunchtime there are always good home-made soups, Ploughman's lunches, a super steak and kidney pie plus 2 daily specials and basket meals. In the evenings the steaks are the speciality of the house but that does not preclude them from serving veal, fish and vegetarian dishes. The sweets are limited but there is a bottomless coffee pot and wine is available by the glass or bottle. This is a true pub giving value for money.

USEFUL INFORMATION

OPEN: 12-2.30pm. (3pm-summer) 6.30-11.00pm Food: 12-2.15pm 7-9.15pm Closed Mon lunch in Win.

CHILDREN: Well behaved children welcome

CREDIT CARDS: None taken

LICENSED: Full licence

GARDEN: Yes, benches at front, Walled water garden.

RESTAURANT: Quality English fare Good pub food, excellent steaks

BAR FOOD: As above

VEGETARIAN: Usually 2 dishes

ACCESS FOR THE DISABLED: Regrettably none

34, Gloucester Road,
Cirencester, Gloucestershire
Tel: (0285) 653892

THE DRILLMANS ARMS
Public House

Right in the heart of the Cotswolds at Cirencester, on the main Gloucester road, is a splendid pub, The Drillmans Arms. This 200 year old establishment is deservedly popular. When you are in the bar look around and see if you can spot one of the many regular customers, an eighty three years young man who has been visiting the pub twice a day for more years than most of us can remember. He likes nothing better than to tell people his interesting tales.

Richard and Denise Selby are your hosts here; a very professional couple who exude warmth and hospitality. They are assisted by two teenage sons and three lively bar ladies. You will find the whole atmosphere of The Drillmans Arms is lively, full of fun and good humour. The locals love it and so will any stranger who has the good sense to make it a port of call. Richard is a Real Ale enthusiast so you can always be sure of a good pint.

The food is simple, straightforward home cooking with a variety of dishes available everyday. In addition, the menu has a wide choice including Basket Meals, Chilli Con Carne, Curries, Sandwiches, Ploughmans, Jacket Potatoes and salads. Whilst no specific vegetarian dishes are produced something can always be ordered which will fit the bill. You can eat at The Drillmans Arms seven days a week and always get a good meal at a very reasonable price.

USEFUL INFORMATION

OPEN: Mon-Fri:11-2.30pm.
6-11.00pm Sat:11-11.00pm
Sun:12-3.00pm, 7-10.30pm
CHILDREN: Yes, in Family room
CREDIT CARDS: None taken
LICENSED: Real Ale, Wide variety
lagers, beers, wines & spirits
GARDEN: Patio seating in courtyard

RESTAURANT: Good home cooking
at reasonable prices
BAR FOOD: Wide choice
VEGETARIAN: No, but salads &
sandwiches are available
ACCESS FOR THE DISABLED:
Level entrance

THE TROUT INN

Public House

St Johns Bridge,
Lechlade, Gloucestershire
Tel: (0367) 52313

This is one of those wonderful ancient inns that simply fills you with pleasure from the moment you arrive. Going back as far as 1220 the old wooden bridge over the Thames at Lechlade was replaced by a stone one, and for the housing of workmen entrusted with the building of this, a hospital or Almshouse, dedicated to St John the Baptist was founded by Peter Fitzherbert. In 1472 the main Priory was dissolved by Edward IV, but the Almshouse continued as an Inn known as 'Ye Sygne of St John Baptist Head' until 1704, when the name was changed to the Trout Inn.

Ancient fishery rights granted by Royal charter to the Brethren are still held by the inn, which controls two miles of Trout and Coarse fishing waters. Over 700 years' tradition of hospitality is faithfully maintained today, with the choice to dine and drink in the Candlelit Restaurant or the attractive bars. The restaurant is open Thursday, Friday and Saturday for dinner and a comprehensive bar menu is available every morning and evening.

The garden lawn, stretching from the Creel Bar and Marquee to the edge of the Weir Trout Pool, provides a charming setting for refreshments in the open air during the summer months. You can play Boule or the old Oxfordshire game of 'Aunt Sally'. It is a superb setting for functions. There is a jazz night every Tuesday. The food is excellent: Cook's 'Specials' are available every day. The local trout is tremendously popular as are the many dishes served. Vegetarians are well catered for and for those who enjoy real bread and butter pudding or treacle tart, you are in for a treat.

USEFUL INFORMATION

OPEN: 10-3.00pm, 6-11.00pm.
Summer: All day Sun:
12-3.00pm, 7-10.30pm
CHILDREN: Yes. Separate rooms,
Garden
CREDIT CARDS: Visa
LICENSED: Full Licence
GARDEN: Large garden to Weir
Pool. Marquee.

RESTAURANT: Home-made
changing menu. Cooks specials
BAR FOOD: Home-made, varied &
interesting
VEGETARIAN: Four dishes
ACCESS FOR THE DISABLED: No.

Upper Oddington,
Moreton-in-Marsh,
Gloucestershire

Tel: (0451) 30584

THE HORSE AND GROOM

Inn

There are many delightful hostelries in Gloucestershire but this pretty 16th-century inn built of warm Cotswold stone is one of the most welcoming with its inglenooks and beamed ceilings. Upper Oddington is a charming village sitting on the outskirts of Moreton-in Marsh with the Horse and Groom right in the centre, very much part of village life. It is a place to meet your friends for a drink and a bar meal at lunch time or dine in the attractive restaurant any day of the week. It is also a good pub in which to stay offering 4 doubles, 2 twins and a family room at very reasonable prices. Situated as it is not only are you right in the Cotswolds but also in easy reach of Cheltenham, Gloucester, Bath and Oxford. Children are especially welcome and they revel in the large beer garden with its stream, fish ponds play area and aviary. Rusell and Tina Gainford with Stephen and Alison run this happy establishment together with an excellent chef and a friendly staff.

The food is good quality traditional English with some favourite continental dishes. At lunch time there are not only deliciously filled fresh sandwiches and other bar food but daily blackboard specials which are very tempting. Lamb and cherry casserole is an example or perhaps plaice stuffed with prawns. Vegetarians are well catered for with dishes such as broccoli and cheese mornay. From 7-9pm daily, you can dine well in the restaurant from a menu which has something that will please everyone. The dishes are imaginative and beautifully presented with a wine list that complements the food.

USEFUL INFORMATION

OPEN: Bar meals: 12-2.00pm 6.30-9.30pm. Restaurant: 7-9.00pm daily
CHILDREN: Very welcome
CREDIT CARDS: Access/Visa
LICENSED: Full Licence
GARDEN: Large beer garden, stream, ponds, play area

RESTAURANT: High quality traditional English & Continental.
BAR FOOD: Good range. Blackboard specials
VEGETARIAN: Several dishes daily
ACCESS FOR THE DISABLED: Level entrance

THE ROSE AND CROWN
Inn

Nympsfield, Stonehouse,
Gloucestershire
Tel: (0453) 860240

Situated at the top of the Cotswold hills between Dursley and Nailsworth is the picturesque, unspoilt Cotswold-stone village of Nympsfield. At the centre of village life is The Rose and Crown with the proprietors, Bob and Linda Woodman who have been here for eight years, first as tenants but two years ago they bought it from Whitbread and have since made a lot of improvements including: exposing the Cotswold stone walls and the original fireplaces. It is a truly welcoming inn which is a gathering point for the closely knit village community, and has a growing number of outsiders who have found, and delighted in, the hospitality of the Rose and Crown.

Right through the summer and well into the autumn there are masses of hanging baskets overflowing with flowers, carefully looked after by landlady, Linda. Inside, Bob is ready to serve you with an array of brews including Old Spot, from nearby Uley Brewery, winner of a Camra award. When dining you will be presented with a wonderful menu including many old favourites, some of which you will not know but are well worth sampling. There are Beef and Ale stew, Murphy's Delight, home-made faggots, cod, scampi, sole, prawns, sizzling curries, spicy Goulash, steaks, giant sausages or perhaps one of the biggest Ploughmans you will find anywhere in the district. The bar menu contains over 40 items and there is a special Childrens menu. Sunday lunch is a feast but served only if it has been pre-booked, otherwise the normal bar menu is available. It is a marvellous place to lunch, dine, have a snack or even just a drink enabling you to enjoy the atmosphere of the pub.

USEFUL INFORMATION

OPEN: 11.30-2.30pm, 6-11.00pm
CHILDREN: To eat only
CREDIT CARDS: Visa/Access
LICENSED: Full Licence. 2 bars
GARDEN: Beer garden to side of pub

RESTAURANT: Not applicable
BAR FOOD: Home-made dishes.
Over 40 items on the menu
VEGETARIAN: 5 dishes
ACCESS FOR THE DISABLED:
Level entrance

Oakridge Lynchm Nr. Stroud,
Gloucestershire
Tel: (028576) 371

THE BUTCHERS ARMS
Public House & Restaurant

Two brothers, Peter and Brian Coupe, own The Butchers Arms situated on the edge of the village, tucked away in the beautiful south Cotswolds. Oakridge is unspoiled and 'off the beaten track', approximately halfway between Stroud and Cirencester. It is best to leave the A419 at Brimscombe and then turn right just before Bisley, approaching Oakridge through the winding country lanes.

Documents dated 1836 describe the premises as 'shops and brewhouses; at one time it was thought to be used as a butchers slaughter house also. It is a typical Cotswold stone building with exposed stone and original beams. In the winter there are three blazing log fires, and in summer the large Beer Garden is a delightful place to sit and drink. There is no problem with car parking and you will find that an interesting cross section of people come to enjoy the friendly atmosphere. The Butchers Arms is famous in the area for the quality traditional ales, which is Peter's department, whilst brother Brian oversees the excellent catering.

In the bar you can choose from the lunchtime menu of traditional pub fare such as Stout Beef Pie, Cottage Pie or Cauliflower Cheese, all home made, of course, or from a range of crispy salads and ploughmans, and freshly baked filled baguettes. A Blackboard also features special daily dishes. The Stable Room Restaurant opens Wednesdays-Saturday evenings inclusive and on Sundays at lunchtime, and has a fixed menu of interesting home cooked meals with fabulous puddings and desserts. In addition a blackboard features an ever changing variety of special dishes. Sunday Brunch has become very popular, and there is always a traditional roast on offer.

USEFUL INFORMATION

OPEN: Food: 12-2.00pm,
7.30-9.45pm. Sun: 12-2.00pm.
Pub: 12-3.00pm, 6-11.00pm. Sun:
7-10.30pm
CHILDREN: Small room for children
CREDIT CARDS: Visa/Mastercard
LICENSED: Full Licence.
GARDEN: Attractive large garden

RESTAURANT: Variety, Quality
value for money Reservations
welcome – advisable for
Saturday and Sunday.
BAR FOOD: Home made daily
specials
VEGETARIAN: Yes, one or two
dishes
ACCESS FOR THE DISABLED: Yes,
only from rear

THE COUNTRY ELEPHANT
Restaurant

New Street, Painswick,
Stroud, Gloucestershire
Tel: (0452) 813564

Ken and Marril Gibson are the owners of this delightful restaurant. Chance brought them into catering in 1969. Ken had been an engineer and Marril an actress before they launched their first successful catering venture, cooking for society functions in Kent, Surrey and Sussex, as well as being engaged as Diplomatic Caterers to the Canadian High Commission in London amongst many prestigeous contracts. They have owned the Country Elephant for seven years. It is located in the centre of this lovely village which is known as 'The Queen of the Cotswolds'. The restaurant is only a minutes walk away from the churchyard with its famous 99 Yew Trees.

The Country Elephant, on the ground floor of a Georgian Grade II listed building, has been established for over 20 years. Entry is up a passage which opens out into a large patio with seating for 20, leading to a wonderful, 75 yards long, walled garden. Inside, the cosy Cotswold stone bar exhibits a unique collection of original 'Pont' of Punch cartoons, highlighting "Occasions in history, when wine was drunk in celebration."

Eating here is a comfortable experience, whether it is to enjoy one of the Brasserie type lunches from Wednesdays to Saturdays, a stylish dinner from the superb a la carte menu from Tuesday to Saturdays, or Sunday luncheon, in which great care is taken in presenting one 1st class joint of meat with an alternative fish dish. Interesting vegetarian dishes are always available. The Gibsons specialise in fresh vegetables and old fashioned hot puddings as well as cold desserts. Cream teas are a new feature in 1991. There is a very friendly atmosphere.

USEFUL INFORMATION

OPEN: Lunch: Wed-Sun:
12.30-2.00pm Dinner: Tues-Sat:
7-10.00pm
CHILDREN: Yes. No high chairs
CREDIT CARDS: Visa/Access/
Diners
LICENSED: Restaurant Licence

GARDEN: Yes. Safe for children.
Fan-tailed pigeons kept in
dove-cote.
RESTAURANT: A menu with a
difference
BAR FOOD: Not Applicable
VEGETARIAN: 4 dishes
ACCESS FOR THE DISABLED: No
but help provided

Market Square,
Stow-on-the-Wold,
Gloucestershire

Tel: (0451) 30364

THE KING'S ARMS
Inn/Hotel

If you like places of historical interest you will enjoy visiting The King's Arms which was first licensed in 1548. The first thing you will notice, apart from the mellow yellow Cotswold stone of the building, is the royal coat of arms of King Charles I which sits proudly over the door. The King lodged here in 1645. Inside the sense of history has not been disturbed. The main ground floor bar is super, with exposed beams and roaring open fires to welcome the traveller on a cold winter's day.

Alf Glazebrook and Sandra Marshall have been here for a couple of years now and they have carefully refurbished the restaurant, the resident's lounge and the bedrooms giving them all a quiet air of granduer, in keeping with the age of the establishment. It is a welcoming Inn with a friendly staff, attentive service and a reputation for the quality of the food. There is a car park and well behaved children are very welcome to eat or to stay with their parents in the comfortable bedrooms. You can have excellent bar meals either at lunch time or in the evening. The restaurant, which is upstairs, opens only in the evenings seven days a week. The dishes on offer, either in the bar or the restaurant, will please everyone. The prices are extremely reasonable too. The lunchtime blackboard specials change daily but there is always good traditional English fare. Steak and kidney pie takes on a new meaning here. Dining in the restaurant gives you an excellent choice with the emphasis perhaps on the quality of the steaks and the mixed grills, not forgetting the mouth watering desserts oin the sweet trolley.

USEFUL INFORMATION

OPEN: 11-3.00pm, 5.30-11.00pm
CHILDREN: Well behaved welcome
CREDIT CARDS: Access/Visa/
Amex
LICENSED: Full Licence
GARDEN: No

RESTAURANT: Evenings only – 7
days
BAR FOOD: Wide range lunch &
evening
VEGETARIAN: Various dishes
available
ACCESS FOR THE DISABLED:
Level entrance to bar

THE TROUBLE HOUSE INN

Inn

Cirencester Road,
Near Tetbury, Gloucestershire
Tel: (0666) 502206

On the A 433 between Tetbury and Cirencester, just two miles out of Tetbury, is this charming country pub with the curious name. The 17th-century Trouble House is an inn with a long history of struggle and strife. One landlord hung himself as a result of spending too much money rebuilding it; the next one took it over in a half completed state, but similar financial misfortunes overtook him and he drowned himself. If that was not enough trouble, then the inn was the scene of an agricultural riot in 1830, and centuries earlier the site was the very spot where more than one skirmish took place during the civil war between Royalists and Parliamentarians.

Today, it is a peaceful, welcoming hostelry owned by Mr and Mrs Robins, who have been there for 18 years, and before them an uncle was the landlord for fifteen years. The only link with the troubled past is a friendly lady ghost in a blue dress. Inside, the pub is traditional and furnished comfortably. The ideal place to sup a drink whilst you wait for one of the tasty home made dishes on offer at lunchtime, or perhaps a succulent steak at night. The menu includes a delicious old timer beer and beef casserole or an equally good one using lamb and leek. There are salads and various snacks as well. At night, in addition to steaks, gammon, chicken kiev and the like, there are very good Indian curries served from 7-9pm. Do not expect cooked meals on Sundays when only salads and snacks are served.

USEFUL INFORMATION

OPEN: Mon-Sat: 11-2.30pm,
6-11.00pm Sun: 12-2.30pm,
7-10.30pm
CHILDREN: Yes. Large Garden &
field to play in.
CREDIT CARDS: None taken
LICENSED: Full Licence
GARDEN: Garden tables & see-saw

RESTAURANT: Not applicable
BAR FOOD: Home cooked
VEGETARIAN: 4 dishes
ACCESS FOR THE DISABLED:
Level entrance. Not applicable

The market town of Dunster

INDEX TO PLACES AND VENUES

Leisure in Print Publications

24-26 George Place, Stonehouse, Plymouth Devon PL1 3NY
Tel: (0752) 265956/7   Fax. (0752) 603588

Dear Reader

Lunching out is becoming increasingly popular and it was with this in mind that I was asked to write this book. The venues chosen are varied and I hope you will enjoy them.

It would make the next edition much easier if you would help by suggesting places in which to eat and perhaps where you have been before or after lunch.

I enjoy corresponding with my readers and look forward to hearing from you.

Bon appetit!

Yours sincerely,

Joy David

Joy David